London ...
The Sinister Side

Steve Jones

INTRODUCTION

'London the Sinister Side' was originally intended to be a souvenir guide for travellers who take the Tragical History Tours 'Bus Trip to Murder'. However, during the research I found the subject matter so interesting that I felt it may well appeal to the "armchair" audience too. As a result the guide has been written for anyone interested in the darker areas of London's past.

The events featured are complete and independent and in the order that the bus travels in London . . . through the East End, under the Blackwall Tunnel to Woolwich and Greenwich, returning via Tower Bridge to the Temple.

Tragical History Tours Limited organised their first tour in 1985. My Brother Michael, a former London Teacher, was fascinated by the macabre mysteries and murders in his home town. There was no tour company catering for the darker side of London life. After many months research which included visiting haunted houses and pubs, the scenes of the Ripper murders and reading up on poltergeists the Company was finally launched in June. The first bus tour set out into the backstreets of the East End with only two passengers on board! They were on the trail of Jack the Ripper, the Poltergeist of Bethnal Green, the Phantom Hitch-hiker of Blackwall Tunnel and many more. Since that time the company has rapidly expanded and we now run every night of the week in Summer and most nights in Winter.

Dare you join us on the Bus or in the safety of your own home on a Trip to Murder in London . . . The Sinister Side.

First published in 1986 by
Tragical History Tours (Publications) Limited

This Edition
Wicked Publications
222, Highbury Road, Bulwell, Nottingham NG6 9FE England.
Telephone: 0115 975 6828

© **Steve Jones 1986**

Second Edition (revised) 1987

Third Edition (revised) 1988

Fourth Edition (revised) 1989

Fifth Edition (revised) 1990

Sixth Edition (revised) 1991

Seventh Edition (revised) 1992

Eighth Edition (reprinted) 1992

Ninth Edition (revised) 1993

Tenth Edition (reprinted) 1994

Eleventh Edition (reprinted) 1995

By the same author as

London Through the Keyhole

Wicked London

Capital Punishments

In Darkest London

ISBN 1 870000 04 8

Typeset and printed in Great Britain by
J. W. Brown (Printers) Limited, Darwin Press
77a Blackheath Road, Greenwich, London SE10 8PD
Telephone: 0181-691 1357

CONTENTS

ILLUSTRATION ACKNOWLEDGEMENTS

Many thanks are given to the following for permission to reproduce their pictures:

DAVE JORDAN AND LINDA HELLENS
1, 10, 29, 30, 31c, 51, 53, 63, 64, 65, 67, 68, 69, 70, 71, 72, 84, 103.

MARY EVANS PICTURE LIBRARY
6, 9, 12, 18, 19, 21, 35, 39, 52, 59a, 76, 77, 88, 89, 90, 91, 92, 94, 95, 96, 98, 99, 100, 102.

BBC HULTON PICTURE LIBRARY
11, 13, 14, 16, 23, 24, 28, 38, 40, 43, 44, 45, 54, 59.

THE CITY OF LONDON POLICE
15, 36, 46, 47, 48, 55.

THE NATIONAL PORTRAIT GALLERY
31a, 31b, 56, 57, 74, 75, 104.

GREENWICH LIBRARY
25, 26, 27, 60, 61, 62, 73, (Greenwich Life 1–6) 87.

THE LONDON DUNGEON
3, 101, 105.

THE MANSELL COLLECTION
4, 17, 86, 97.

TOWER HAMLETS LIBRARY
32, 33, 34, 41.

MUSEUM OF LONDON
7.

JANE HAWKES
5.

GUILDHALL LIBRARY
8, 20, 93.

CLEOPATRA'S NEEDLE
3,000 years and miles from home

Carved in 1475 b.c. over 1,000 years before London was named, Cleopatra's Needle is by far the capital's oldest man-made attraction. The giant granite obelisk stands over sixty feet high and weighs in at approximately one hundred and eighty-six tons. Guarded by two lions it stands tall and defiantly on the banks of the Thames thousands of miles from its old spiritual home on the shores of the Mediterranean. It has also brought with it some of the mystery and magic of one of the earth's oldest civilizations.

The obelisk had toppled into the sand near Alexandria and was presented to the British in the early eighteen hundreds. There are at least six men who must have wished the granite had been left to rest in the sands of its homeland and an unknown number of suicides, who maybe fatally attracted by this mysterious stone, have thrown themselves into the river here. It is also the haunt of two of London's ghosts!

It seems the stone did not really wish to leave its warm homeland, bringing the Pharaohs, albeit in symbol form to the damp, foggy climes of Northern Europe. Because of transportation problems the obelisk was not brought to England until 1878. Loaded onto an iron pontoon it showed its obvious displeasure at being moved from its homeland by nearly drowning off The Bay of Biscay. The obelisk was saved but six seamen died in a ferocious storm.

What stories it could have told if erected in its originally intended location, eavesdropping in front of the Houses of Parliament. If the obelisk were ever to return to its homeland, historians would have an interesting time sifting through the odd collection of articles buried underneath. These include an 1878 newspaper, four bibles in different languages, a railway guide, a razor and pictures of the twelve most beautiful women of the day. Cleopatra's Needle appears a rather cold and lonely monument, and it may be this isolation, on the foggy banks of the river that makes it the most popular suicide spot on this stretch of the Thames.

These suicides are probably in some way connected with the two ghosts spotted in this area. One is a hazy troubled figure seen standing on the wall apparently deliberating as to whether to jump. When approached he invariably takes the plunge, the body disappearing before the water is reached. You might like to keep an eye out for the second ghost: a completely naked figure dashes out of the shadows and dives into the river, though once again a splash has never been heard.

One cannot help but feel that the needle is waiting for the day when it can return home and stand proud under the hot Egyptian sun.

One of the most popular suicide spots on the Thames

THE TEMPLE
A garden of roses

Just a few hundred yards down river from Cleopatra's Needle we come to the old western end of the City, Temple Bar. It was in the gardens here that the roses—either red or white—were first picked, leading to the long and bloody civil war between the Yorkists and Lancastrians, The War of the Roses. The Temple was first mentioned in 1293 as a chain between two wooden posts, and it grew in importance as a gateway until finally being redesigned by Sir Christopher Wren. It was not only a gateway, however, but also the public place of exhibition of the bodies, in particular the heads, of traitors to the state.

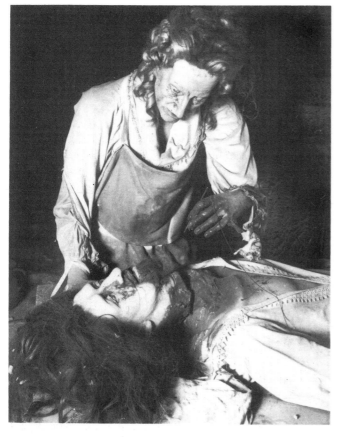

3. Sewing back the head of Charles I after his execution (From the London Dungeon)

Exactly who the traitors were of course depended on who inhabited the corridors of power at any one time. The incidence of executions was brought to a head, dare we say, during and after the civil war. The King himself, Charles I, was executed in 1649, the head later being sewn back on but exactly twelve years later to the day the body of Oliver Cromwell, the man ultimately responsible for his death was dug up. Cromwell had never been a particularly popular Lord Protector and the report of his death in the Commonwealth Mercury was ironically followed by an advertisement for a new book by Bunyan:—

'A few sighs from hell or the groans of a damned soul'.

After his death he was crowned like a King and lay in state for three months but on the day of his funeral the only cries heard were those of wild dogs. He had been dead two years but was so reviled by the London mob that his body was never left to lie in peace. Like all traitors he had been made to ride backwards in a cart to Tyburn where he was hanged by the neck 'to the going down of the sun'. After his hanging he was decapitated, his head being dipped in tar and hoisted over Westminster Hall until being blown down in a storm. Rumour has it that the head was picked up by a soldier and secreted in the corner of the chimney in his home.

England was still a divided country long after the civil war and the restoration of the monarchy. More than twenty years after Cromwell's death there was an attempt by some old roundhead soldiers to assassinate William and Mary at The Rye House. The leader was Sir Thomas Armstrong who along with his accomplices was sentenced to death by the notorious Judge Jeffreys. His body was carved up and boiled in salt so that the birds would not consume it. The heads of his co-conspirators were impaled on spikes set on a curved pediment at The Temple. Much to their disgust the heads were looked over by the statues of King Charles the first and second in Roman dress. There was some easy money to be made for anybody with a telescope, as these were hired out at ½d a time so inquisitive onlookers could get a close-up of the grisly scene. One character even started firing ballbearings from his crossbow using the heads as targets. One of the skulls is reported to have stayed up for thirty years before being blown down in a gale.

The old Temple Bar, designed by Wren, was removed to Hertfordshire in the last century as it was an impediment to the traffic. There has been talk for a long time of bringing it back to London once a suitable site can be found. The Temple area today is dominated by the legal profession and not surprisingly has a legal ghost of its own. Hanging Hawkins (Sir Henry Hawkins) who is most often seen at midnight wearing a wig and robes and carrying a bundle of papers under his arm.

The Strand, just up the road from the Temple, was the scene of a cold-blooded murder more likely to be witnessed in a James Bond movie than in the streets of London. This is the tragic story of the murder of Georgi Markov who defected from the East and sought political asylum in 1969. On several occasions he had expressed fear of the Bulgarian secret police to his wife, after his writings and broadcasts had angered the communist world. Just after 6 o'clock on 7th September, 1978 Markov was walking along the Strand on his way to work when he felt a brief stinging sensation in the back of his right thigh. He thought it had come from an umbrella prod by a man standing in a bus queue. The man, speaking with a foreign accent, apologised, hailed a taxi and disappeared. Markov's leg started to stiffen and feeling feverish he went home five hours later at 11 p.m. His white blood corpuscle count soared from 10,600 to 26,300 in one day and despite massive antibiotic injections he died two days later.

At the inquest it was discovered that Markov had been murdered by ricin poison which comes from the castor oil plant. This white poison had been administered in a metal pellet and later tests carried out with the substance on a live pig showed the animal develop the same symptoms as the murdered writer.

Nobody was ever brought to trial for the crime and there is no direct evidence linking the Bulgarian Secret Service but in cases like this the truth has a way of willing out over a period of time.

SWEENEY TODD THE BARBER
Purveyor of cannibalistic pastry

Probably the best known resident of Fleet Street was Sweeney Todd, the demon barber. Few customers having a shave at number 186 lived to tell just how close it was. The barber's shop had a chair specially fitted with a tilting mechanism so that the unsuspecting traveller, settling back to enjoy the smooth cut of sharpened razor over lathered face, was suddenly tilted through the trap door and down into the cellar below. If this fall did not kill him Todd was quickly down, razor in hand, to finish off the job. G. K. Chesterton summed up Todd's modus operandi very succinctly with the lines;

"The trap he set for customers was Sweeney's little joke;
when the buyer found the cellar,
the cellar found him broke".

It seems there was a motive other than bloodlust in the killings; an underground passage led to Mrs. Lovatt's cellar in Bell Yard. She was a pastry cook and her meat pies were held high in esteem by her many customers who included several workers from the nearby courts of justice. Little did they know they were eating the evidence.

Speaking of evidence there is very little to support the existence of the character Sweeney Todd, as there are no reports of his capture in any newspapers and it is likely that the story is based on the french equivalent of a 'Penny Dreadful'. There is however an interesting little twentieth century adjoiner to the story of the demon barber. In 1949 a demolition worker at 154 Fleet Street found a sign marked 'Sweeney Todd the Barber' and on further investigation found a trap door. He must have been in high hopes of clearing up the mystery as to the myth or reality of the purveyor of cannibalisitic pastry. What he had in fact discovered were the premises of a barber whose name appeared in the London telephone directory ten years earlier—Sweeney Todd the barber. The name still lives on, not only in Stephen Sondheim's admirable opera but also in London rhyming slang: Sweeney Todd—Flying squad.

There have been stories of cannibalism throughout history and unfortunately this is not just a crime of the past. I relate here briefly two accounts of this ghastly crime; for a third, please see the section on Jack the Ripper. These stories are not for those of you with delicate stomachs or just about to have a meal. Here are the stories of Sawney Bean and Joachim Kroll, neither of them fictitious.

Sawney Bean lived in a cave in Galloway (Scotland) with his wife, eight sons, six daughters and thirty two incestuous grandchildren. They lived by hunting, though not normal game—they preyed upon human flesh, murdering travellers going to and coming from Edinburgh. It is estimated that they cannibalized fifty people a year making up a total of 1,500 murder victims. One man managed to escape and raise the alarm but could do nothing to prevent his wife being dragged from her horse, having her throat cut and being instantly cannibalized.

The King determined to wipe out this monster and took four hundred men and several bloodhounds to the coast. They tracked down Bean and family to a cave where limbs and torsos of victims 'were hung up in rows like dried beef'. The family were captured after a long battle and burned at the stake. A witness named Nicholson wrote that;

'they all in general died without the least drop of repentance . . . but continued cursing and venting the most dreadful imprecations to the very last gasp of life'.

Cannibalism did not die out with the Beans or the Todds but continued very much into the twentieth century, with Joachim Kroll being arrested as recently as 1976. Kroll was a mentally sub-normal living in Germany. In his flat he kept rubber dolls, which he used to strangle with one hand whilst masturbating with the other. Between 1959 and 1976 he killed at least fourteen young girls or women and removed portions of each victims body to eat, having a preference for the buttocks and thighs of young girls. You might say he was caught red-handed as when the police raided his flat they found a stew bubbling and amongst the carrots and potatoes, a child's hand. Other parts of the body were found in the deep freeze; When questioned about them Kroll said he thought he might as well save money on meat.

After reading the above two accounts Sweeney Todd does not seem to be such a demon especially as it is ninety percent certain he was a fictitious character.

THE MAN IN GREY
(London's popular Theatre ghost).

Just up the road from The Temple is the home of another bewigged and berobed ghost: The Theatre Royal, Drury Lane. It has witnessed the making of much theatrical history including David Garrick's stage debut and the first production of Sherridan's 'School for Scandal'. But it also has a more turbulent history, having been burnt down twice and seen several riots and assassination attempts on the lives of King George the first and third. It should hardly come as any surprise that this is the home of London's most seen and famous theatre ghost—The Man in Grey.

Unlike some of his ghost brothers and sisters his sighting does not create an atmosphere of chill and fear but is welcomed by producers as he is most often seen during the run of a successful production. His name comes from the grey riding coat in which he appears, (almost always during the matinee) and his powdered wig and three-cornered hat were once witnessed before a full audience. His route does not vary, materialising at the end of row D he moves along the back of the Upper Circle, passes the bar and vanishes through a wall on the far side of the auditorium. The Man in Grey demands that his privacy be respected, as if you attempt to approach him his outline blurs, his features become indistinct and he disappears. He seems to have a particular penchant towards musicals and has often been seen during such musicals as 'The King and I', 'Oklahoma' and 'South Pacific'.

Just who is this hit-loving fearless ghost, once sighted going about his business in the full fury of an air raid? In the last century workmen discovered a hollow piece of wall occupied by a skeleton near the start of the Man in Grey's walk. A dagger was lodged between its ribs and fragments of a richly braided cloth were also found attached to the bones. It has been speculated that the ghost was a wealthy newcomer to London during the reign of Queen Anne. This man may have attracted an actress and been stabbed by a previous lover, the body not being discovered for one hundred and fifty years. We shall never know for certain the identity of this popular figure though there are many anxious producers and actors who would dearly love him to pop up in the cast again, albeit unannounced.

THE PLAGUE 1664–5
Bring out your dead

4. London street scene during The Plague

London has had a history of plagues dating back over one thousand years before the Great Plague killed off an estimated one hundred thousand of the capital's population. There is no doubt that the sanitary habits of the middle ages contributed to the spread of the earlier plagues. Latrines were built over rivers and it was not uncommon for the river Fleet to stop flowing because of the sheer volume of human waste, rakers being employed to clean the 'toilets'. Swift and Steele wrote of The River Fleet in The Tatler;

"Now from all parts the swelling kennels flow,
And bear their trophies with them as they go:
Filth of all hues and odours seem to tell
What street they sail'd from, by their sight and smell . . .
Sweepings from butchers' stalls, dung, guts and blood
Drown'd puppies, shaking sprats, all drenched in mud,
Dead cats and turnip tops, come tumbling down the flood."

The first public convenience was not introduced into London until 1852 when in Fleet Street the price to pee was 2p. Quite a common site in the middle ages was the human public convenience! This was a man wearing a large cloak and carrying a pail, the cloak being used to conceal the customer as he relieved himself in the bucket. Stones, shells, bunches of herbs and sponges on sticks were employed before the adoption of toilet paper.

5. The human public convenience

6. Man being bled

Some resourceful peddlars became rich by selling potions of pepper, urine and salt as a cure. Others offered crude surgery and bleeding though none of the courses were successful. To make matters worse all dogs and cats were ordered to be killed; they were cornered and clubbed within five days, thus eliminating the best natural deterrent to the carrier of the plague: the rat.

Human bodies were left in the street for two or three days and the carcasses of dogs, cats, pigs and horses swelled up and burst under the summer sun. The heavy sweet smell of putrefaction hung over London and for those who tried to escape the capital, life was equally difficult, as when they approached towns outside London they were met by guards and pelted with stones or manure.

The plague started in the hot summer of 1664 with large swarms of flies and ants adding to the general conditions of squalor. It came to a head in 1665 and then disappeared almost as suddenly as it had arrived. The Great Fire of London the following year helped to ensure that the Plague would not return with anywhere near as much ferocity ever again.

Sanitary conditions were not much better in 1665 when the Great Plague took a grip in Drury Lane. Many including the Royal Family left London, though Samuel Pepys stayed throughout to give us an accurate account of the happenings. The first signs of the plague were a swelling of the lymph nodes in the groin or armpit, shivering, vomiting, splitting headaches and an intolerance to light. Doctors used to visit households covered from head to foot with a large beak containing herbs and spices to protect them from the stench. Once the plague was diagnosed everybody in the house, contaminated or not, was locked in for forty days and if another death occurred in the house the quarantine period had to start again. Quite often fathers could not stand to see their families die in such awful conditions, the air heavy with the smell of vomit and excretia. They would put great pressure on the guards to let them out and if they did not comply would attack them with ropes dropped from an upstairs window, hoping to strangle them. Red crosses painted on the doors of the contaminated houses were to be seen all over the city and the familiar cry 'bring out your dead' heard in the deserted streets. Old women were employed as 'searchers of the dead' and they had to search the body to find the cause of death. Such was the anarchy of these times that nurses would sometimes strangle their charges for their clothes. Unemployed servants were used to drive death carts, but because of their volume the carcasses were buried just inches below the ground. London was in a state of semi-anarchy as drunken gravediggers tried to keep up with demand. Bearers sometimes wheeled bodies around shouting out such cries as 'faggots, faggots! five for sixpence.' They would hold up the bodies of young children as if they were butcher meat and it was not uncommon for the bodies of young women to be undressed and the cart drivers perform necrophile.

7. Plague doctor: The beak was filled with herbs and spices to protect him from the stench

9

LONDON BRIDGE
"As fine as London Bridge"

By far and away the oldest bridge across the Thames, London Bridge has a unique history, being the only crossing point until 1749. A second bridge was long overdue as there is a report of a three hours traffic jam on the crossing in that very year.

The first bridge, made of wood, was built by the Romans awaiting the arrival of Claudius. The site was chosen because of the gravel on the North side (near the present St. Paul's) and the sand on the south side being able to support the structure above the marshes. Whether this bridge lasted until the Eleventh Century or whether it was repaired or rebuilt we do not know but London Bridge was mentioned again in 1014. Ethelred, trying to regain his throne from Canute called on the aid of Olaf of Norway. During the night Olaf's vikings lashed ropes around the supports of the bridge and set off downstream with the tide; the foundations were shaken and the bridge gave way thus dividing the Danish forces. The popular nursery rhyme 'London Bridge is falling down' is probably based on this event, being adapted from an old poem by Ottar Svarts which begins;

> 'London Bridge is broken down
> Gold is won and bright renown.'

In 1212 fire broke out on the bridge and sightseers and firefighters were trapped in the middle as the fire caught hold at both ends of the bridge. A witness to the ensuing catastrophe, a man named Stow, recorded what happened next.

> 'Then came there to aid them many ships and vessels into which the multitude so inadvisedly rushed that, through fire and shipwreck, three thousand people were killed.'

An extraordinary challenge took place on London Bridge in 1390 more like a scene from Sir Walter Scott than real life. On St. George's Day a joust was held between Lord Welles of England and David de Lindsey of Scotland to determine whether the English or the Scottish Knights were the more valiant. Lances in hand they approached each other at full gallop from opposite sides of the bridge. The Scot, de Lindsey won at the third tilt and true to the age of chivalry ran to help his opponent until a doctor arrived.

De Lindsey and Welles became good friends, the Scot visiting the Englishman in hospital every day until he recovered.

There was a drawbridge which was raised when there was a great threat to the Capital and many bloody battles were fought on this road to power. Jack Cade, 'the bastard of Falconbridge' and his supporters fought a fierce battle with the citizens of London, the houses on the bridge being set alight and women with their children jumping in the river to save themselves.

The southern approach to the bridge was known as Traitors Gate where the heads of enemies of the state were placed on spikes. In 1598 a German visitor counted over thirty heads. They had been parboiled in one of the gatehouse rooms and dipped into tar to preserve them. The heads exhibited included those of Jack Cade, Sir Thomas More, John Fisher and the conspirators in the gunpowder plot. The heads of the two persecuted for their religious beliefs, both impaled on the same stake, finally found very different resting grounds, Sir Thomas More's head was acquired by his daughter and later buried at St. Dunstan's, Canterbury. Bishop Fisher's head was thrown into the Thames a fortnight after his execution, as instead of rotting it was growing fairer by the day! At about the same time as these executions some Germans working in London started to use the skulls as cups hoping that this would cure illness . . . it didn't and most of the imbibers died a short while later.

The bridge was considered a prime place to live and amongst its inhabitants was the artist Hogarth whose excellent illustrations are featured in this guide. He would not have had far to go for his shopping as the bridge was full of all kinds of shops including hosiers and shoemakers.

The last London Bridge, like Cleopatra's Needle, has made a long journey overseas, this time to warmer climes. It can now be seen in Lake Havasu, Arizona; though whether the buyers thought they were purchasing Tower Bridge is a matter of conjecture.

8. Heads of traitors at the entrance to the bridge

ST. PAUL'S CATHEDRAL

The fascinating story of the building of the present day St. Paul's has been recounted many times. What is less well-known is the fact that this is the fifth church of that name to stand on the site and if anything the fourth St. Pauls was even more awe-inspiring.

This was a most remarkable building being considerably larger than todays which in its time had the tallest spire ever built. It was not however so much a church, more a gigantic meeting and market place and in 1598 Bishop Bancroft was told St. Paul's was:

> . . . 'A common passage and thoroughfare for all kinds of burden bearing people such as Colliers with sacks of coal . . . also a daily receptacle for rogues and beggars however diseased, to the great offence of religious minded people.'

Because of its size, St. Paul's proved to be a very heavy burden on the Exchequer and when the spire was struck by lightning in 1447, it took many years to replace. Events took place there which we would associate more today with circuses than churches. In 1660 an amazing horse, Morocco (a middle sized bay English gelding shod with silver) was brought to the Cathedral. Morocco could count and perform tricks and together with his master he climbed the steps to the top of the tower to the delight of 'a number of asses' who brayed below. (It is not clear whether this quote refers to the human or animal population). It seems street entertainers had an even harder time in those days than they do today . . . performing a similar feat in Rome they were both arrested and burnt as wizards. Many rope dancing feats were performed at the church and the day before Queen Mary's coronation she saw a Dutchman standing on the weathercock of the steeple waving a five yard streamer.

St. Paul's was divided into different areas. Many of the poor would congregate around Duke Humphrey's tomb to wait for a free dinner. If you dined with Duke Humphrey it signified you had passed the day with an empty belly. In other areas people used to gather to look for work or to buy and sell all kinds of merchandise—ranging from pamphlets through to pies.

Despite the fact that Henry VIII gambled away the church bells on a single throw of the dice (they were removed and sold for the value of the metal), St. Paul's did occasionally serve its religious purpose. New translations of the bible, along with Luther's works, were burnt here and in 1517 a maypole was denounced to death, although whether the sentence was carried out is uncertain.

The mid-seventeenth century saw the demise and eventual destruction of the fourth St. Paul's. The demise started in the Civil War. Cromwell's troops burnt the pews and furniture and the roof fell in after the scaffolding was sold. The nave was used as a cavalry barracks and during the bitter winter of 1652 horse dung was sold as fuel at 4d and 6d a bushel. For a small fee young trouble makers could climb to the top of the church and shout abuse and throw stones at passers-by. It seems hooliganism is not just a twentieth-century phenomenon. The destruction came in 1666; the church—by then in a very dilapidated state, being razed to the ground in the Great Fire.

9. The old St. Paul's, not so much a church, more a way of life

The present St. Paul's is one of the best known landmarks and one of the finest works of architecture in the capital. The church was protected in the Second World War from the Luftwaffe's bombardment by volunteers of St. Paul's watch who defused incendiary bombs and mines. The church amazingly experiencing very little damage.

Not surprisingly St Paul's has a ghost, sighted by many churchmen. It takes the form of an elderly clergyman and emits a high-pitched tuneless whistle. He haunts the west end of the Cathedral where a secret stairway has subsequently been discovered.

Millions of people around the world will have witnessed the Royal Wedding of Prince Charles and Lady Diana in 1981. Luckily the bells were in good working order as, unknown to the many viewers, is the old legend—that if anything goes wrong with the bells it is considered an ill-omen for the Royal Family.

10. (Overleaf). The present St. Paul's haunted by an elderly clergyman on a secret stairway

CABLE STREET AND SIDNEY STREET

11. *Police were captured and temporarily imprisoned*

All police leave was cancelled and mounted police sent to the area. Roughly 300,000 people were waiting for the fascists who were assembling in Royal Mint Street. There was a massive police presence and drawing their batons they managed to make some headway through the masses so that the fascists could march. At Gardeners Court however, there was a solid human mass jamming the streets chanting;

"They shall not pass"

With the aid of trams road blocks were set up.

There was another route via Cable Street although this was known as a tough area. A barricade with the contents of a builder's yard was erected to block the street. Marbles were thrown under horses hooves and paving stones and bricks thrown at the police. The windows and roofs were crowded with women hurling bottles down at anybody in uniform. The area quickly became polluted by the smell of old sauce and vinegar bottles. The battle raged on. Police were captured and temporarily imprisoned in shops. Barricades were broken down only to see new ones replace them a little further along the road. The police finally admitted defeat and the march through the East End had to be abandoned.

The Mayor of Stepney later said;

'I have never seen the people of East London so thoroughly aroused and angry during the whole of my experience'.

The next weekend the fascists returned and smashed the windows of all the Jewish shops in the Mile End Road. The abandonment of the march however saw the start of the decline of the blackshirts and they were never again to march in uniform in such force.

Germany was not the only country with a fascist movement supported by blackshirted 'troops' demonstrating against the Jewish population. Britain's fascist party was led by Sir Oswald Mosley and used to parade through the East End in the thirties rhythmically chanting anti-Jewish slogans.

They chose this area of London because half of the Jewish population in the whole of Britain lived here. For their protection the marchers were surrounded by large groups of police and there was a feeling, rightly or wrongly, that they were acting in collusion with the fascists. If anybody protested against the blackshirts they were often pounced upon and charged. Mosley's supporters used to smash and burn Jewish shops and it was not uncommon for their owners to be followed into the backstreets and beaten up.

On Sunday, 4th October, 1936 Mosley announced a major East London rally, inviting blackshirts in uniform from all over England to the East End. He was to inspect the troops and march along Commercial Road through the heart of the East End. Attempts by local mayors and one hundred thousand signatures collected by the Jewish Peoples Council against fascism failed to get the march banned. The London Communist Party and the Independent Labour Party issued a call to block the march at Gardners Corner and Cable Street. The East End walls were daubed with white paint;

"all out on 4 October"

12. *A strategic retreat*

THE SIDNEY STREET SIEGE

13. **X** *marks the rooms occupied by the gang*

There was another battle fought in the East End near Commercial Street a quarter of a century earlier and this one involved no less a person than the young Winston Churchill, the then Home Secretary.

On the night of December 16th, 1910 police were summoned to a jeweller's shop in Houndsditch after a constable had heard movement within. They went to a side door of the building next to the jewellers and knocked. They were all astonished to hear gunshots as a man ran out firing a revolver, three policemen being killed instantly and two others badly wounded. The gunman and his two accomplices fled, leaving behind the tools they had been using to bore into the jewellers. The next day a doctor was summoned to a house off the Commercial Road and he found there a man with a bullet in his back; returning later he found the man to be dead. The doctor had noticed two men of foreign appearance leaving the house and reported the whole affair to the police.

After the attempted revolution in Russia in 1905 many Russian immigrants had settled in the East End and the police had reason to believe that they were mixed up in the deaths of the policemen and the man subsequently found dead from the gun wound. The man they wanted most to interview was Peter Piatkow, known as Peter the Painter. They traced his whereabouts seventeen days later to a house in Sidney Street between Commercial Road and Whitechapel Road. Police surrounded the house and Churchill ordered a detatchment of Scots Guards to be in attendance in case of emergency. Churchill concerned himself personally with the affair and there is a famous photograph taken of him sheltering in a doorway, observing the events.

There were two men inside the house assumed to be Peter Piatkow and a man known as 'Fritz'. For five hours the two men fired at the police before finally setting fire to the house, continuing to shoot whilst the house burnt around them. It was only when the roof fell in that the shooting ceased. When police finally gained entry they found the bodies so charred that they could not be positively identified, nor was it possible to link them with the Houndsditch murders. Winston Churchill was later to give evidence in court on what happened during the siege.

Thankfully this has been one of the very few 'shoot-outs' in the Capital.

14. *The fire was so fierce, the bodies could not be identified*

15. *The young Winston Churchill at Sidney Street*

16. *Police at the scene armed with shotguns*

PRISON LIFE

17. *Prisoners working at the tread-wheel, and others exercising, in the 3rd yard of the vagrants' prison, Coldbath Fields*

*"As he went through Cold Bath Fields he saw
A solitary cell;
And the devil was pleased, for it gave him a hint
For improving his prisons in Hell."*
Coleridge.

If life was hard on the streets in the East End in the last century, life in prison was bordering upon hell. Upon entry, prisoners' hair was cropped— without the use of a comb— and they were dressed in dirty grey jackets and knicker-bockers with one standard size in underwear. In many prisons, including Newgate silence was the rule. Prisoners slept on planks in undecorated cells and toiled at monotonous work all day long. Most prisoners were engaged in oakum picking; that is, unpicking old tarred ships' ropes over one inch thick, so that the strands could be re-spun and used again.

Offenders within the prison were often whipped or put in a strait-jacket or did two shifts of three hours on the treadmill. This was a machine invented by a Lowestoft engineer, William Cubitt. The screw or prison officer would turn the key and everyone had to start the uphill march; twenty-four steps and then another twenty-four and so on. The prisoners kept their balance by holding on to a handrail and by the end of their daily stint they had each done

the equivalent of climbing the Matterhorn. In some prisons the mill was used to raise water but in others it had no practical use and many women would deliberately injure themselves so they could go to the prison hospital to escape the monotony of the wheel. Another form of hard labour consisted of moving 24lb cannon balls from one side of a room to the other and then back again; this procedure continued without respite for up to seventy-five minutes.

Prison food was often inedible with very little change of diet. Indeed prisoners meals consisted of only six different foodstuffs; bread, gruel, potatoes, meat, soup and cocoa. Much of the gruel, or stirabout as it was known, was refused, even though the prisoners were very hungry. The bread was stale and potatoes full of black disease; the meat was so bad that prisoners held their noses when eating it. To find black beetles in the greasy meat or vegetable soup was a common occurrence and one welcomed by some prisoners as most ate them along with any weeds they could find—and the prisoners were so hungry they often supplemented their diet with wax candles.

Reforms have come slowly over the years but even today in London, Victorian prisons are still in use and catering for more people than originally intended.

THE FLEET PRISON
The Gaol of London

Two prisons were built in London in the twelfth century whose very mention would strike terror into the hearts of both criminals and debtors alike. In the early days of The Fleet roughly half the prisoners were held for non-payment of debt, this figure rising later to a staggering ninety per cent. If the law were brought back today would there be anyone left outside?.

Built in the years around 1130 Fleet prison had a long history of corruption. The post of keeper of the prison was much sought after, having many financial perks—prisoners could pay to stay away for days on end and better accommodation could be found for a price. The post of keeper was hereditary and it stayed in one family for over three hundred and fifty years. In the early 1700's the post changed hands for £5,000—a staggering figure for those days.

In earlier times several people were imprisoned there for their religious beliefs and it was not uncommon for people to be put in the pillory, branded, have their noses mutilated and ears cut off. The torture instruments included the thumbscrew and an iron collar, put on so tight that some prisoners suffocated to death.

The prison was always the target for rebels and revolutionaries and was burned down and reconstructed three times over the centuries. Conditions were so bad that in the 1690's Moses Pitt described the dungeon he shared with twenty other prisoners as:—

> *"so lowsie that as they either walked or sat down you might have picked lice off their garments".*

A dungeon called the strongroom was used as a place of punishment. Made of rough unplastered brick the strongroom had no chimney or fireplace and there was no light except that which came over the door. The whole area was damp and stank, standing right next to the dunghill for the whole prison. It was common practice to leave here dead bodies awaiting burial, alonside the living.

In 1729 the warder was put on trial for murder as six men in his charge had died because of the atrocious conditions. He was later acquitted.

Astonishingly it appears that no record was kept of the prisoners admitted and the number of prisoners escaping were too numerous to count.

The Fleet prison was demolished in 1846.

18. Whipping for minor offences was common

NEWGATE—THE ENGLISH BASTILLE

'A Prototype of Hell'.

Until its demolition at the turn of the century the name Newgate was synonomous with death and deprivation. The prison is mentioned in the twelfth century in the Newgate Calendar. A record of executions and crimes, it was a best seller throughout the last century, being the only book ,along with The Bible, kept in many homes. Daniel Defoe, Titus Oates and Lord Gordon were among the many well-known public figures who experienced the atrocious conditions of what was probably London's most corrupt prison. All necessities, such as beds, had to be paid for and your treatment and conditions depended entirely on how much money you had or could get hold of. Henry Fielding called it one of the most expensive places on earth, indeed not unlike some of London's hotels today! If you happened to have a private income a place was found in the Press Yard where the rooms were large and spacious as well as being well supplied with light and air, and free from smells. The prisoners confined here spent much of their time drinking, gambling and gossiping. There were inns both inside and outside the prison gates and outsiders were allowed in to mix and drink with the prisoners. It would not be uncommon to witness a game of skittles or tennis or even be a party to one of the many illicit weddings performed 'inside'.

For the majority of prisoners however, life was not so comfortable. Defoe who, as we know, had first hand experience of the gaol captured the atmosphere of the surroundings in Moll Flanders;

> *"The hellish noise, the roaring swelling and clamour, the stench and nastiness....an emblem of hell itself."*

The stench in the prison was so bad that during sessions herbs were strewn in the court of justice and the passages leading to them from the prison. To help prevent infection and disguise the obnoxious smell of the prisoners they were bathed in vinegar before their appearance in court. When they arrived they would often swear and spit at the judge who needed protection not only from the venom of their attack but also their physical state which after a period of confinement in the prison was appalling, ventilation being almost non-existent.

Upon entry prisoners were robbed of everything they possessed, including their clothes and left to fend for themselves as best they could. The women in Newgate numbered approximately one hundred in 1808 and were packed in like slaves in the hold of a slave-ship. The prison reformer Mrs. Fry described the women as:

> *"swearing, fighting, gaming, singing, dancing, drinking and dressing up in men's clothes."*

Newgate became famous principally however, because this was the prison from which most prisoners set out on their last journey on this earth. Many were taken in the earlier days the two and a half miles to Tyburn, the place of execution was later changed to Newgate itself. It cannot have been very reassuring to condemned men on their last night to read the inscription on the gateway to their cells. This started with the lines;

> *"You prisoners within who for your wickedness and sin After many mercies showed you are now appointed to be executed to death tomorrow in the forenoon".*

Condemned prisoners were forced to attend the last sermon with their coffin at their feet during the service. The actual executions are described in the section of that name. Newgate was demolished in 1902 to make way for the Old Bailey, many of the same bricks being used in both buildings. Just before demolition the old rooms were thrown open to the public and the seats and benches sold for firewood. The dock was sold for £10 and the grating used in Jack Shepherd's escape fetched £7 10s.

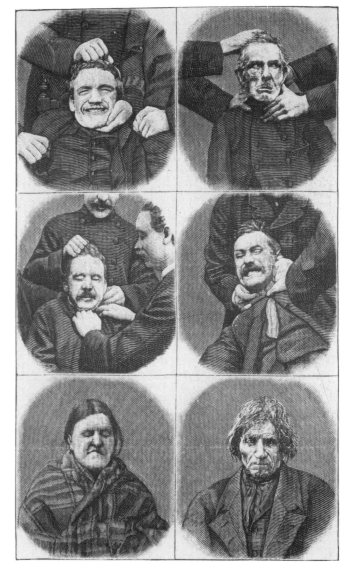

19. The early days of police photography. some of the convicts seem somewhat shy

ELIZABETH BROWNRIGG, SARAH MALCOLM AND ELIZA FENNING
(The ugly, The bad and The good)

ELIZABETH BROWNRIGG

Murder was certainly not confined to the male sex and the three cases chosen here all end up with the murderess being hanged. One can have very little sympathy for two of the women concerned, but there are grave doubts as to the culpability of the third who was to wear her wedding dress—not to the aisle as intended—but to the gallows.

One of the most hated women ever to be hanged was Elizabeth Brownrigg who occupied a house in Fetter Lane. She was married to a painter and was the mother to some sixteen children. Her job was as a midwife but her name was to become synonymous with sadism and cruelty due to the manner in which she treated her 'servants'. She was the midwife to St. Dunstans workhouse and abused her position to entice young girls back to her house on the corner of Fleur de Lys court. Nearly all the girls were orphans or of low intelligence or handicapped in some way. Two girls were kept in the cellar for more than a year, grinding colours for their master. They shared this cellar with hogs, both feeding and drinking from the same trough.

20. *Elizabeth Brownrigg, stripped her servants and flogged them to death. She is urged on by the devil.*

A True representation of the Horrid Cruelty's Committed by ELIZ.ᵗ BROWNRIGG on the Body of MARY CLIFFORD her Apprentice the 31 of July 1767 for which the Aforesaid Eliz.ᵗ Brownrigg was Executed at Tyburn Sep.ᵗ 14

21. Mrs. Elizabeth Brownrigg awaiting execution, she shows no signs of remorse

The girls did not see a bed throughout the year and the eldest who was seventeen lost her ability to speak, her head swelled up to an enormous size and her eyes became almost imperceptible. The younger girl who was thirteen testified that after the whippings, the blood which streamed from their wounds formed puddles underneath them where they sat in the cellar. The seventeen year old died in St. Bartholomews hospital. Mrs. Brownrigg had made their life hell, hanging them from the waterpipe by their wrists (stripped naked) and whipping them until the sadistic mistress had to pause from sheer exhaustion. At other times they would be imprisoned in a cold cellar with a chain around their neck tightened to the point of suffocation, staying there for days being fed only on bread and water. One girl had her tongue cut through with a pair of scissors. The beatings from canes, horsewhips and brooms took their toll on the girls and two died before the authorities arrived. They were just in time to save one poor wretch who had been whipped so fanatically that her clothes had to be removed by a surgeon, so deeply had they cut into the body.

Cries were heard from the cellar grate to the side of the court and eventually the authorities were informed and after a long chase Mrs. Brownrigg was captured and sentenced to death. One curious feature of the case was that her son and husband who played no inconsiderable part in the murders both recieved sentences of under one year in prison. Elizabeth Brownrigg showed no signs of remorse whatsoever in prison and she was cursed all the way to the gallows, the women shouting;

> 'Pull her hat off, pull off her hat that we may see the b......s face'.

A writer of the time summed up the case saying:

> 'She whipped two female 'prentices to death,
> and hid them in the coal-hole..
> For this act,
> Did Brownrigg swing.'

After her hanging on 14th September 1767 her body was dissected by the Royal College of Physicians.

SARAH MALCOLM

Some thirty five years before Elizabeth Brownrigg was to make her final ride to the gallows, there was a rather strange case of triple murder at the Temple. The accused in this case was Sarah Malcolm, a charwoman who strangled both her employer and her companion and to avoid anyone giving evidence against her cut the maidservant's throat. These murders were not perpetrated for sadistic reasons but for the old evil: greed. The case was peculiar for a number of reasons, not least of which was that the stolen money, £53, was found hidden in Sarah's hair. She was duly convicted and sentenced to hang for the murder of the three women. Two days before her hanging, Hogarth came to the Fleet prison to draw her likeness, he later said she was capable of any wickedness. She was hanged between Mitre Court and Fetter Lane, her cheeks painted for the occasion. The hangman was John Hooper, nicknamed Laughing Jack for the quips he used to make to the convicted prisoner. We shall never know if they found them amusing. The case aroused considerable interest amongst the general London folk and people paid to see the corpse at the undertakers. A gentleman in mourning even gave half-a-crown to kiss the body. Her confession was sold in pamphlet form and her skeleton exhibited at the botanical garden in Cambridge.

There was no doubt as to the guilt of Sarah Malcolm and Elizabeth Brownrigg and they were both duly jeered and stoned on their way to execution. The case of poor Eliza Fenning would not have reached the courtroom today so circumstantial was the evidence and nobody reading her story would be in any doubt of her innocence.

ELIZA FENNING

In 1815 a young attractive servant girl, Eliza Fenning was 'caught' partly dressed, going into the room of two apprentices lodged in the same house, that of Mr. and Mrs. Turner. She was severely admonished for this 'crime' and the prosecution stated that from this day she held a grudge against her master and mistress and was determined to get her revenge. A short time later, the family fell violently ill after a meal prepared by Eliza (which she incidentally had eaten herself). The meal in question was dumplings which were black and heavy and had not risen as they should have done. The prosecution alleged that Eliza had added arsenic to the meal, this being kept in the kitchen as rat poison. The only evidence they had was the testimony from Mrs. Turner that Eliza had specifically asked to do the cooking on the day in question. Even though there were no deaths, the charge of attempted murder was still punishable by death. The case was held before the violent Sir John (Black Jack) Sylvester. The defence was a disgrace not mentioning that the yeast had remained unattended for some time and the fact that the girl had eaten the dumplings herself. At no time was it ever proved that the sick people were suffering from arsenical poisoning. Eliza was convicted after a one-sided summing up of the case and was *carried from the box convulsed with agony and uttering frightful screams* All she could say after the trial was *'I am truly innocent of the whole charge—indeed I am. I liked my place, and I was very comfortable'*. Many people at the time thought her innocent but the minds of the people were more occupied with the battle of Waterloo and the war with France. On the eve of the day she was due to marry, Eliza Fenning went to the gallows in the white muslin gown she should have married in the following morning. She was one of the prettiest and bravest women to face the drop and she aroused the sympathy of all in attendance, with her white dress—the high waist tied with a satin ribbon and high laced lilac boots. She stood proud and calm—until the hangman tried to fit the mandatory cap over her face so that the crowd would not see her convulsions. Because of her hat, the cap would not fit, so the hangman took a dirty handkerchief from his pocket to cover her face. Eliza objected strongly to the priest who was on hand but the dirty rag had to stay. Eliza's final words were *'I am innocent'*.

22. Sarah Malcolm (left), days before her execution. Her skeleton was exhibited in the Botanical Gardens in Cambridge.

23. Brunel on board the Great Eastern shortly before he had his stroke—he is second from the right.

24. The ship was jinxed and haunted throughout its turbulent life

THE GREAT EASTERN AND PRINCESS ALICE

For centuries London was an important centre for shipbuilding and it was at Millwall docks on the Isle of Dogs that the largest ship ever built until that time, The Great Eastern was constructed. From the start, the ship was dogged by bad luck; some may say jinxed. Designed by Brunel, the ship, seven hundred feet in length, was completed after three years work in 1857, but its construction had claimed lives in somewhat mysterious circumstances. One boy fell and was impaled on a scaffolding support, a sightseer was killed when a monkey wrench dropped by a workman above fell on his head, and a third workman disappeared without trace; that is until some thirty years later, but not let's jump our story.

Because she was too large to be launched in the normal manner The Great Eastern had to be eased sideways into the river. Brunel had asked for a quiet launching so that shouted orders between workers on the barges and in the docks could be heard. Much to his annoyance the directors sold thousands of tickets to see the launching of the world's largest ship. Because of the large crowd there was a breakdown in communication and the ship moved only a few feet and stuck. A panic ensued and the bargemen fled in fear of their lives lest the ship came crashing down on them and it was here that the ship claimed a fourth life when a windlass tossed a worker into the air. He later died from his injuries.

The ship was to stay stuck for the next three months.

For the maiden voyage Brunel came aboard to select cabins but only after a few minutes suffered a stroke from which he was later to die. On its first trip the paddle wheel boilers blew up killing six stokers. In its short life there were four mutinies on board and she served as a floating circus.

The crew somehow knew when danger was approaching as just before any disasters, of which there were many, there was a warning, a kind of knocking that was never explained. On the way to the breakers yard after a troubled life the hammering was heard once again. During the dismantling a skeleton and a bag of rusty tools were found trapped between two layers of metal, the mystery of the missing ship-builder had been revealed. Had he been trying to communicate with the captain with his hammer?

THE PRINCESS ALICE

'Hoy, Hoy, Where are you coming to'
(Cry heard from one ship to the other just before the accident)

The Londoners had enjoyed their day out, the trip down river on the pleasure steamer had been a success and despite the overcrowding (between 700 and 900 were on a boat equipped for only 500) passengers sang and danced to the sound of mouth organs and concertinas. It was a rare treat for a party of invalids and the highlight of the year — 1878, for a bible class of 50 youngsters. Picnic hampers lay empty as the sun started to set. Six out of seven aboard were not to see it rise again as they were shortly to be involved in the greatest single disaster in the history of the Thames.

It can only have been at the last minute that out of the gloom, anybody saw the collier Bywell Castle—an iron ship five times the weight of the Princess Alice. The collier hit the starboard side almost cutting the paddle-steamer in two; she then drew back and the filthy waters of the Thames flooded into the Princess Alice. There was a violent shuddering and the paddle-boat broke in half and the boilers burst. The bow and stern rose skywards. Bodies jammed in the doorways in the mad rush to escape, were found still wedged together when the Princess Alice was later raised. Not all was panic however as survivors later told of two clergymen who calmly met their fate singing hymns as the water rushed in.

The chance of survival for those who managed to escape the boat were not great. Pathetic cries were heard from the river; the most pitiful being:
"Twenty pounds to save my life".

One woman used her parasol as a lifebuoy and others used their huge skirts and petticoats to float to the banks. The Captain of the Princess Alice, Captain Grinstead was last seen clinging to the rail of his ship, going down with his charge. 32 survivors were rescued by the Bywell Castle and when she dropped anchor another 12 people who had been clinging to her sides were swept to their deaths. Anybody with a small boat went to the scene to drag the survivors into their vessels and they were later paid five shillings for each body recovered, often fighting each other in the search for the carcases. As might have been guessed from the readings of this guide the bodies were not left in peace as all jewellery and wedding rings were stolen and pickpockets later preyed on the mourning relatives.

All in all over 600 people may have perished in the disaster, 120 of them being buried at Woolwich. There was a lengthy inquest into the disaster, with blame alternately being put on both vessels. Finally it was decided that the Princess Alice was not properly and efficiently manned and the number of people on board was more than was prudent. The means of saving life on board the Princess Alice were also insufficient for a vessel of her class.

Galleons Reach, the site of the accident was afterwards known as Haunted Reach and just four years later, the Bywell Castle disappeared without trace on her journey home from the Mediterranean.

25. The Bywell Castle crashing into the pleasure steamer, Princess Alice off Galleons Reach, Woolwich.

26. *Souvenirs of the Thames Catastrophe*

27. The search for the bodies

FOUNDERING OF
THE PRINCESS ALICE

William Digby Seymour, QC,LL.D
Temple, September 11, 1878

*   *   *   *   *

There's a rippling wave and a sparkling spray
as the fair ship steams along:
It is seemly to close the festive day,
With the measures of dance and song —
But, ah! those lips will be silent soon,
And the music hushed in that bright saloon.

As they're wafted to shore on the evening breeze,
How happy those voices sound!
There is nothing the listening ear can please
Like a pleasure-boat homeward bound.
There is laughter on deck — there is love below —
Ah! little their danger the doomed ones know!

They are midway now, on the Thames' broad stream,
And above them a clear, calm sky:
Hark! heard you not then a dismal scream,
And the shouts — as of agony?

The river runs — but the music's gone —
Two ships have met — and there floats but one!

Oh! weep for the fate that befel the gay,
For the young who too early died,
For manhood and beauty swept away
By that cold, unpitying tide!
Weep for fond bosoms forced to part,
For the desolate home, and the broken heart!

And weep for that frenzied last embrace,
Round the covering infant press'd —
Ah! take the slime from her pallid face,
And the lifeless babe from her breast!
And weep for the minstrel mute and chill,
For the shattered harp that's for ever still.

Yet work while ye weep! on the saved attend,
Your solace the orphans crave;
To the friendless give — what he lost — a friend;
To the drowned — what they want — a grave!
Oh! Woolwich — they deeds in these late sad hours
Point stranger to Heaven than all thy towers!

It is sweet when the Royal Lady sends
Her message of Queenly love;
It is sweeter when faith with a prayer ascends
To a higher throne above.
May He who the issues of life controls
Have mercy on those eight hundred souls.

THE MYSTERY OF JACK THE STRIPPER

The Thames probably gets its name from old English meaning dark river, but until the massive increase in population in the 1800's, the river was not as polluted as one might have suspected. A whale fifty-eight feet in length was killed between Deptford and Greenwich in 1658 and just over a hundred years later a two toothed cachalot, twenty-one feet in length, was taken above London Bridge.

The river has always been a hive of activity, bustling with vessels of all shapes and sizes; prison boats, sailboats and small purl-boats weaving their way in and out selling nips of whiskey to the sailors. Dishonesty and corruption were the order of the day as thieves swarmed over the ships at night stealing anything and everything—including the ship's anchor. Many children were used as smugglers; others were sent into the river at low tide for pieces of coal, rope, cable or old iron. The young lads often injured their feet in the cold water and this must have been one of the most wretched ways of making a living.

Before the new London Bridge was built, the Thames used to freeze over and frost fairs were held on the ice, with plenty of food and drink and amusements to entertain the locals. In one year however there came a sudden thaw and the ice gave way throwing hundreds into the river, some of them meeting a watery grave. Benjamin Franklin swam the Thames from Chelsea to Blackfriars, but it is certainly not recommended today.

In early Victorian times the colour of the river varied between dark green and black—and in the hot dry summer of 1858, known as the Great Stink, the curtains in the Houses of Parliament had to be soaked in chloride of lime to repel the smell.

Water.—In 1858, the water had become very impure by the sewer-water emptying itself into the Thames, and the sulphate of lime in it causing an insufferable stench, the chloride of sodium denoting its origin among the human habitations on the banks of the river; added to which were the organic matters. Man pours into the Thames the refuse of a hundred towns and villages, besides the washings of manured lands, before it gets to Teddington Lock. The water, already impure, is taken at the rate of 100,000,000 of gallons a day, and after washing London and its inhabitants, inside and out, is again returned to the Thames, bearing with it the vegetable and animal refuse of dwelling-houses, mews, cow and slaughter-houses, and all sorts of manufactories in which organic matter are used.—

(*Dr. Lankester*). In the following year, 1859, the cleansing of the Thames by disinfectants was commenced; and during the season there were employed about 4,281 tons of chalk-lime, 478 tons of chloride of lime, and 56 tons of carbolic acid, at a cost of 17,733*l*.

Timbs—"*Curiosities of London*".

Rivers have often been dumping grounds for murder victims and with the Thames being a tidal river floating past so many back gardens, it is no wonder that the police and seamen occasionally came across the odd floating corpse. In the last century, Mrs. Dyer, a baby farmer, strangled and threw into the river the bodies of forty-six of the babies she had been paid to adopt, while an Irishwoman, Kate Webster dismembered her mistress, whose pieces she threw into the Thames. One of the most horrific series of murders connected with the river and still unsolved began comparatively recently. 2nd February, 1964

A body fished out of the Thames looked worthy of close examination. The female form was naked save a pair of stockings around the ankles and knickers stuffed into the mouth. This was the start of a little publicised police hunt into a series of vicious sexual murders that were never to be solved, the murderer being given the name 'Jack the Stripper'.

The woman found in the river was named Hanna Tailford and an open verdict recorded on her death. When a second body was found two months later, only three hundred yards from where the first had been fished out, the police started going through their files and found that two similar deaths had been recorded in 1959 and 1963. All the women were prostitutes, all under 5' 2" and the latest, Irene Lockwood was four months pregnant. Irene who specialised in snatching wallets from her clients as they took their trousers off, died from drowning.

The first body found away from the river a little later that year was that of Helen Bartholowmey, who was found naked with four teeth missing one being lodged in her throat. The teeth had all been forced out and upon examination sperm was found at the back of her mouth. She may have performed fellatio on the last customer before she was murdered, but more likely, she had been orally raped. Two coffee cups were found in her room and the record player left playing.

Two more bodies were found in quick succession, both bearing the hallmarks of a sadistic sexual attacker. Mary Fleming's false teeth were missing from her body and sperm was found in her throat, as was the case with Margaret McCowan. The police had by now gathered some clues, as traces of paint were found at the scene of the latest three murders.

The murders continued into 1965 with Bridie O'Hara, found dead in Acton in a kneeling position, her teeth having been removed after death with once again, sperm found in her throat, By now police had found a disused warehouse near a paint spray shop and an analysis of the paint showed it was of the same kind as that found at the scene of the murders. A list of twenty workers was reduced to three—and just as in the Ripper case a leading suspect, (a security guard who worked nights) committed suicide, leaving a note to say he could not bear the strain anymore. Although the murders ceased the man's guilt was never proved—and the murders are still unsolved!

THE KRAY TWINS
'The Sun ain't gonna shine any more'

28. Reggie and Ronnie Kray, the twin brothers who ruled the East End in the fifties and sixties

Ronnie and Reggie Kray were born in the East End in 1933. The both became professional boxers before turning to professional crime. Emerging from national service where they spent a great deal of their time in the guardhouse they became nightclub bouncers and both very ambitious, they moved into the protection racket whilst opening a billiard hall in Mile End Road. In many areas in East London they just used to turn up and say they were the new bosses and on the rare occasions anybody disputed the fact they were quickly and viciously dealt with. One man who placed his hand on Ronnie's shoulder and said that he was getting fat needed seventy stitches and Ronnie often used to slash people with a razor just for the hell of it. In the fifties , Ronnie led an attack on a man named Martin who had lost favour with the twins the victim being taken to hospital with a bayonet wound from one of Ronnie's accomplices. For his part in the attack Ronnie was sentenced to three years imprisonment which he found very difficult to face, being transferred to Epsom mental hospital. The twins were somehow growing apart. Ronnie was a homosexual and had a strong dislike of women; Reggie married. The observations about Ronnie's weight were true, though I certainly wouldn't have mentioned the fact. Reggie seemed to be the calm thinker and Ronnie the rather dangerous and unstable eccentric, collecting a vast arsenal of guns and taking the nickname of the colonel. The twins were not slow to exploit their similarity to each other and even swopped places in the mental hospital, Ronnie walking out after Reggie had

changed positions with him! There was nothing the police could do though later Ronnie gave himself up and served out his sentence.

The twins opened restaurants and nightclubs and were often seen mixing with show biz stars and politicians and indeed they were mentioned in the House of Lords in 1965. Lord Boothby brought up their case asking how much longer were they going to be held without trial after being charged with demanding money with menaces. They were both later acquitted after ninety days.

Anyone who knew Ronnie at that time would not have been surprised when he committed his first murder. Indeed his own brothers words upon hearing the news were 'Ronnie does some funny things'. The murder took place at the Blind Beggar on Whitechapel Road. A rival gang to the Krays from South London had just lost their two leaders, the Richardson brothers to lengthy spells in prison and one of the gang, still at liberty had dared to cross the river and was drinking on the Kray's doorstep. In fact Ronnie was in a pub only half a mile away when he heard the news. The unfortunate man was a certain George Cornell who had taunted Ronnie about his boyfriends and the fact that he was a homosexual. He had even warned the parents of Ronnie's boyfriend about the nature of their relationship.

Ronnie, with his accomplice John Barrie entered the pub at 8.30 p.m. and Barrie fired shots into the ceiling. Cornell looked up from his drink and said 'well just look who's here'. These were to be his last words as Ronnie shot him through the eye, the bullet coming out through the back of the neck.

With the words from the Walker Brothers' hit 'The sun ain't gonna shine anymore' stuck on the jukebox, Ronnie Kray and John Barrie left the pub, Ronnie remarking that dead men don't tell tales. As we have seen, murder was not an uncommon crime in London but this kind of Chicago gangland killing in front of witnesses was very rare and shocked the East End. Such was the brothers' reputation that the police could not find anybody to act as a witness, the barmaid saying she was in the cellar at the time of the incident.

From that time on Ronnie goaded his brother Reggie about never having committed a murder and so almost at random they chose a victim for the twin brother. The unfortunate person this time was Jack "the Hat" McVitie—he always wore a hat to cover his baldness. His crime; he was said to have made some satirical remarks about the brothers! He was lured to a basement flat in Stoke Newington but not all went to plan, the gun misfiring twice, once from each brother. They had to stab McVitie to death in a very clumsy and messy murder with the knife blade passing right through McVitie's neck into the floorboards. The body was never found. Reggie was heard to say after the murder 'you want to try it sometime it's a nice feeling'.

The crimes were becoming too blatant and a squad was formed, headed by John DuRose specifically to smash the Krays. At dawn on the 8th May, 1968 sixty-eight men made raids on various addresses in the East End and rounded up the gang including the twins. With the twins in custody the barmaid of the Blind Beggar pub acted as a witness for the prosecution and after a forty day trial ten members of the gang were found guilty on various charges and the Krays were sent down for thirty years apiece.

29.   The scene of the murder of George Cornell.

BETHNAL GREEN
A Poltergeist and
Underground Tragedy

31. Right: The Bow Bells pub. Beware of ghostly hands in the ladies loo! ▶

30. Scene of one of the biggest wartime disasters

Moving further East we arrive in Bethnal Green, once a pleasant country area. By Victorian times it had become the poorest district of London. There was an artificial lake of putrefying matter some two hundred and thirty feet long, containing human refuse and the decomposing bodies of cats and dogs. The odour was of the most abominable nature.

Bethnal Green had become famous for cock-fighting, the inhabitants often kept large dogs and bulls were let loose in the streets on a Sunday morning. Would it be any surprise under these conditions if some of the inhabitants acted rather strangely? One resident, crossed in love, indulged in a singular partiality for rats and shut himself up in a house full of these rodents. He taught them tricks and was often seen dancing in their midst.

Many of the thirty thousand killed in the blitz on London in the second world war came from this area as Bethnal Green is in the heart of cockney London and was very densely populated. In March 1943, the local population were expecting a reprisal air-raid after reading of a successful bomb attack on Berlin. In the event of the bombers arriving the people would go to the local underground railway station which served as an air-raid shelter. The only problem was there was only one entrance for ten thousand people!

The alarm sounded at 8.17 p.m. on the 3rd March and large numbers left their homes in haste for the shelter. They were joined by the occupants of two cinemas and three buses emptied their passengers here. In ten minutes 1,500 people had entered the shelter but at 8.27 p.m. a salvo of rockets was discharged from a battery one third of a mile away. Rumour went around that bombs were falling and the crowd surged forward on the nearly dark stairway. Two witnesses saw a woman with a child stumble on the third step from the bottom. Everybody then started to fall on top and there was a jam completely across the full width of the stairway. Seeing the entrance temporarily blocked, more and more people shoved and pushed to get in. There ensued uncontrollable panic with cries and screams; the last breath of life of many being trampled to death underfoot, suffocated. The stairway became a mass of dead and dying bodies pressed together into a tangle of such complexity that the work of extrication was slow and laborious. The last casualty being cleared three hours later.

27 men, 84 women and children had been suffocated.

One of the many Taylor Walker pubs we occasionally use on the tour is The Bow Bells on Bow Road. As with all our stops it has not been chosen by chance. Ladies especially beware! In 1974, a normal toilet visit became anything other than that. Imagine if you can, seeing the locked door open and the toilet being flushed by an unseen hand! The landlord has also seen mist rising from the floor and felt an icy wind. A short time after these bizarre happenings a seance was held to try and contact anybody who may have wished to get in touch and during the seance the toilet door crashed open shattering the glass in the windows!

THE GUN

"And take care of my dear Lady Hamilton, Hardy, take care of poor Lady Hamilton. Kiss me Hardy".

In the 18th century, when the Royal Navy's victualling office was near Tower Bridge, there was a foundry further down the river called Gun Yard which produced cannon that was fired from Nelson's ships at the Battle of the Nile and at Trafalgar.

In those days this stretch of the Thames was known as Gun Shoal, and maps of the period clearly mark the Gun Tavern, Cold Harbour, which was regularly visited by Nelson himself for his assignations with Lady Hamilton.

Upstairs is the very room where he would meet his Emma, to whom he was so devoted that he allowed her to drag him to gambling parties—an activity which he hated and which eventually led to her exile and premature death in France.

But in her heyday Emma Hamilton was a vivacious beauty with a charm that carried her irresistibly from a poor village home to the forefront of London Society. "Indeed she was passed from one husband to another in the payment of a debt". For a time during her liaison with Nelson she lived in a villa in Cold Harbour named Isle House, and there is a story that the lovers sometimes used an underground tunnel between two buildings for clandestine meetings.

Another historic feature of the Gun Tavern is its enclosed staircase with its smuggler's spy-hole cut into one wall. During the Napoleonic wars this concealed window was often used as an observation post in the constant battle of wits against the revenue officers.

The maritime atmosphere of the Gun is maintained to this day by the lightermen, dockers, river police and customs officers who make up the clientele of this famous Taylor Walker house, where the Thames sometimes rises to within inches of the top of its walled courtyard and where the floor obligingly lists nine inches to starboard.

The visitor today may get something of a shock inside the pub as a series of postcards, drawn by prisoners during the last century are not all they seem to be.

31a. Lady Hamilton

31b. Lord Nelson

31c. Used to meet at The Gun pub on the river.

THREE EAST END MURDERS

32. The Murder of the Tavern Keeper's Family.

The East End had long been associated with crime. Maybe this was due to the desperate conditions of poverty, or the fact that here was the docking area for thousands of foreign sailors; strangers of different nationalities would come and go at will. The numerous immigrants, Irish, Jewish and Chinese were also said to be the cause, though there is no evidence to support these allegations. There was no shortage of murder cases even before the arrival of the notorious Jack the Ripper.

The local population was outraged at the gruesome and bloodthirsty Ratcliffe Highway murder in December 1811, two entire families being wiped out. The first victims were Mr. Marr, his young wife, apprentice and baby son whose throat was cut in his cradle. A tavern keeper, his wife and servant girl met the same fate, the girls head almost being severed from the body. The murders were committed with a sailors knife, mallet, chisel and crowbar. The whole of London lived in terror and one shopkeeper sold three hundred alarm rattles in ten hours. The police arrested a sailor named Williams on what would today appear very flimsy evidence and there must be some doubt as to his guilt. We can never be sure as Williams hanged himself from a rafter whilst in police custody. The London mob felt cheated of their revenge, so his body, dressed in white shirt and blue pantaloons and the kerchief he had used to hang himself, was paraded through the streets of Stepney and Wapping. He was accompanied by some three hundred police and in the cart alongside his body lay the murder weapons. The convoy stopped at the sites of the murders before taking him to the corner of Cable Street and Cannon Street Road. Here he was buried in a shallow grave, a stake hammered through his heart.

33. The Italian boy with white mice.

After the trial of the notorious bodysnatchers Burke and Hare, guards were being stationed around the London cemeteries. Instead of snatching bodies from the graves three 'Burkers' Bishop, May and Williams decided to provide their own corpses. They befriended a young Italian boy and fed him rum laced with laudanum. The 14 year old lost consciousness and was hanged upside down in a well, the idea behind this action being two-fold—firstly to kill the boy through drowning, secondly to remove all traces of the rum 'concoction', the murderers callously adjourning to Old Street to drink coffee while the boy drowned. After selling the teeth to a dentist they hawked the body around the London hospitals. They were becoming professional, having already murdered a woman and an 11 year old boy. Carlo Ferrari, the young Italian, was to be their last victim. He had been a popular figure in the East End and used to beg near the Bank with a cage of performing white mice. When he was missed a search was set up and one of the murderer's children was noticed playing with the mice. The garden was dug up and Carlos' clothes found buried there. As with the famous Burke and Hare trial one testified against the other and Bishop and Williams hanged, May was acquitted.

They were hissed and booed on the scaffold and crowd barriers collapsed at the Old Bailey, so incensed was the mob.

Murder was not just confined to the male sex. Eliza Ross, an alcoholic, used to entice old women or young girls to her house in Goodmans yard. They were cold bloodedly murdered and their bodies sold. Those she could not sell she kept in straw in the cellar and gradually disposed of in dust heaps. She used to sell and sometimes wear the victims' clothes—also murdering cats for their skins. Thankfully she was eventually captured.

There were many more cases like these and a general look at conditions in the East End would help us understand the setting of the most brutal and baffling murders London or maybe the world has ever witnessed—the murders of Jack the Ripper.

34. Bishop, Williams and May, murdered the Italian boy to sell his body for dissection.

BISHOP. WILLIAMS. MAY.

THE MURDERERS OF THE ITALIAN BOY.

London : Published by Sears, Charterhouse Square.

CONDITIONS AND PROSTITUTION IN THE EAST END
"Drunk for a penny, dead drunk for tuppence"

Even from Elizabethan times The East End was considered rather dirty and unappealing. The dung, offal, carcasses and entrails from Stretford slaughterhouses were cast into roadside ditches and rivers which later provided drinking water and there was a factory at Wapping to extract alum from urine. It is no surprise that the black death arrived nearly every year.

In the 18th and 19th centuries the population increased dramatically with many Irish (due to crop failure) and many Jews (religious persecution) pouring into the East End. Many of the German, Russian and Polish Jews were unable to speak or read English. The Irish had the habit of leaving bodies in their houses for days after they died and the children used to play with them. Indeed the children did not have so long to live themselves, 55% dying before the age of five.

Drunkeness seems to have been the rule rather than the exception in the poorer districts, the main tipple being gin. This gin was brought from Holland and was free of tax and could be sold without a licence. It was obtainable almost anywhere: barbers, grocers, tobacconists, brothels, prisons and barrows in the street attracted customers with signs such as:

"Drunk for a penny, dead drunk for tuppence"

Gin, cursed Fiend, with Fury fraught,
Make human Race a Prey;
It enters by a deadly Draught,
And steals our Life away.

Virtue and Truth, driv'n to Despair,
Its Rage compels to fly,
But cherishes, with hellish care,
Theft, Murder, Perjury.

Damn'd Cup! that on the Vitals preys,
That liquid Fire contains;
Which Madness to the Heat conveys,
And rolls it thro' the veins.

35. Gin Alley by Hogarth

36. *19th Century East End Slums.*

Gin was later taxed and to combat this, sold under the pseudonyms of 'Ladies' delight' and 'King Theodore of Corsica'. In 1743 one house in eight sold 'Blue Rum' and the average consumption per week including children was about 2 pints. There was very little rest for some, with gin houses doing their best trade between 4 and 8 a.m. Alcohol was not just limited to Gin and the workers in local sugar factories consumed sixteen pints of beer a day.

Western London represented wealth, comfort and luxury whereas the East was associated with poverty, squalour and degredation. The factories spewed out a thick obnoxious fog, as glue was manufactured from boiled blood and bones. The workers in Match factories often suffered from premature baldness and rotting of the jawbone—phossy jaw, caused by phosphorous poisoning. Men were crushed to death in the struggle to get jobs unloading ships and there were bread riots during the severe winters.

People had to make a living as best they could. Some women sieved a livelihood from the mountains of refuse that sprang up on waste ground, sorting out old iron, rags and bones. They stood knee deep in the rubbish they examined, their skirts tucked up under leather aprons. Old men took to gathering dog's dung used in dressing of leather, a bucket full buying a days food and lodging. Some Eastenders took to the sewers, looking around their entrances for coins or anything of value. The sewers were a very dangerous place to be for two reasons; at high tide they used to fill to overflowing so there was always the risk of drowning—and there were rats. Stories of bodies being picked clean to the bone were common and after a pregnant sow fell into the sewers there was a plague of wild pigs raised on garbage.

Life was none too safe above ground either. Cattle drovers used to amuse themselves by deliberately stampeding their herds on the way to Smithfield. The animals took refuge in shops and houses. Live cattle were driven through Sunday congregations before being slaughtered at the market. Blood flowed through the streets and entrails were dumped in the drainage channels. Dickens in 'Oliver Twist' described the market;

"The ground was covered nearly ankle deep with filth and mire: a thick steam perpetually rising from the reeking bodies of the cattle"

There was a lighter side to London life in the nineteenth century. Walking down the street it would not be uncommon to be accosted by beggars, pretending to be either old soldiers or lunatics. There were many street musicians playing deliberately loudly and badly to elicit money for their silence. You could also be entertained by ballad singers who used to sing tunes then sell the sheets. Many of the songs were about murder and execution and several stories were passed down this way.

Commercial Road was the haunt of the street reciter who knew Shakespeare backwards and earned a wage of ten shillings weekly. Street singers sold hot eels, pickled whelks and asses milk, but the most common sale was that of the human body.

37. *Overleaf. East End family at the turn of the century. Notice the shaved head of the father. The mother appears to be expecting again. This was reality for millions of Eastenders and even luxury for some.*

Mayhew, in his famous study of the London Poor interviewed a reverend informant who told him about sleeping arrangements:

"Boys have boastfully carried on loud conversations, and from distant parts of the room, of their triumphs over the virtue of girls, and girls have laughed at and encouraged the recital. Three, four, five, six and even more boys and girls have been packed, head and feet, into one small bed some of them perhaps never met before. On such occasions any clothing seems often enough to be regarded as merely an encumbrance.

Sometimes there are loud quarrels and revilings from the jealousy of boys and girls, and more specially of girls whose 'chaps' have deserted or been inveigled from them. At others, there is an amicable interchange of partners, and next day a resumption of their former relationship . . . Even in some houses considered of the better sort, men and women, husbands and wives, old and young, strangers and acquaintances, sleep in the same apartment, and if they choose, in the same bed. Any remonstrance at some act of gross depravity, on the part of a woman not so utterly hardened as the others, is met with abuse and derision."

Prostitution

It is very hard to put a definite figure on the number of prostitutes working in the East End in the last century but 80,000 is the most quoted number. They worked in parks, passages and lodgings all over the city. Almost half of the girls had at sometime been in domestic service and

38. The same family displaying their worldly goods!

because of the economic circumstances, slipped into prostitution. In the upper classes more attractive street walkers used to go about their business in the West End, a red bandana around their shoulders and a small cane in hand. The older and more wretched graduated to the East End where they drunk enormous amounts of gin and worked to get enough money for a nights accommodation, often in a crowded room, sometimes slumped over a rope for twopence a night.

The 'going rate' varied, depending on the appearance of the prostitute and the affluence of the customer. In the East End, for an attractive woman in her twenties, anything between half-a-crown and ten shillings was the norm. The price was considerably lower for the older gin-sodden women.

The couples would go to a lodging house where the smoking of opium was not uncommon. These houses contained anything up to forty tiny box rooms, separated by deal boards. Each room had a bed whose sheets, and indeed occupants, rarely washed. Mayhew described one womans hands as being 'so black and filthy that mustard and cress might have grown upon them'.

Perhaps the best way of understanding the lot of the prostitute is from the women themselves. These quotes were taken from interviews with Mayhew in the East End in the middle of the last century.

'I aren't happy either. It isn't happiness but I get enough money to keep me in victuals and drink'.

'I don't suppose I'll live much longer and that's another thing that pleases me'.

I know very many sailors—six, eight, ten, oh more than that. They are my husband. I am not married, of course not, but they think me their wife while they are on shore. I do not care much for any of them'.

I was a servant girl away down in Birmingham. I got tired of workin' and slavin' to make a livin', and getting a bad one

39. Ladies of the street.

at that; what o' five pun' a year and yer grub, I'd sooner starve I would'.

Strange things happen to us sometimes, we may now and then die of consumption but the other day a lady friend of mine met a gentleman at Sam's and yesterday morning they were married at St. Georges, Hanover Square. The gentleman had lots of money'.

Prostitutes also used to supplement their income by fleecing their prospective customer:

"The woman walks forward, or loiters about, followed by the men, who are hanging in the rear . . . She picks up a man in the street, possibly the worse for liquor; she enters into conversation, and decoys him to some quiet secluded place, and may there allow him to take liberties with her person, but not to have carnal connection. Meantime, she robs him of his watch, money, or other property, and at once makes off."
'Mayhew—London Labour and The London Poor'.

A German visitor in the 1820's talked about his visits to the theatre; one of the major meeting places in the early part of the century. He said that it was almost impossible to keep off 'the repulsive beings' especially when drunk which was not seldom the case:

In 'London Labour and the London Poor', John Binny described some more dregs of the prostitute class:

. . . Some bloated, dissipated, and brutal in appearance; others pale and wasted by want and suffering. Many of them resort to bilking for a livelihood, that is they inveigle persons to low houses of bad fame, but do not allow them to have criminal dealings with them. Possibly the bodies of some may be covered with dreadful disease, which they take care to conceal. While in these houses they often indulge in the grossest indecencies, too abominable to be mentioned, with old grey-headed men on the very edge of the grave. Many of these women are old convicted thieves of sixty years of age upwards. Strange to say, old men and boys go with these withered crones, and sometimes fashionable gentlemen on a lark are to be seen walking arm in arm with them, and even to enter their houses.

41. Soup Kitchen for the Jewish poor.

40. Street scene: Notice the absence of shoes.

Binny was also interested in the class of prostitutes called soldiers' women:

They are from sixteen to thirty years of age, and several even older. Some have been in the streets for seventeen years and upwards. They live in the greatest poverty, covered with rags and filth, and many of them covered with horrid sores, and eruptions on their body, arms and legs, presenting in many cases a revolting appearance. Many of them have not the delicacy of females and live as pigs in a sty . . . In the middle of the day they sometimes wash their skirt, the only decent garment many of them have—their underclothing being a tissue of rags . . .

Bracebridge Hemyng wrote on Prostitution in 1861:

The soldier cannot afford to employ professional women to gratify his passions, and if he were to do so, he must make the acquaintance of a very low set of women, who in all probability will communicate some infectious disease to him. He feels he is never safe, and is only too pleased to sieze the opportunity of forming an intimacy with a woman who will appreciate him for his own sake, cost him nothing but the trouble of taking her about occasionally, and who, whatever else she may do, will never by any chance infect. I heard that some privates in the Blues and the Brigade of Guards often formed reprehensible connections with women of property, tradesmen's wives and even ladies, who supplied them with money and behaved with the greatest of generosity to them, only stipulating for the preservation of secrecy in their intrigues.

When later the prostitutes were excluded from the theatre they continued to ply their trade outside as well as in the casinos, night houses and pleasure gardens. The Times was forced to note that 'in no capital city of Europe was there daily and nightly such a shameless display of prostitution'. Such was the scene in 1888. Little did the women of the East End know the terror and panic that was to grip the area in the second half of the year.

JACK THE RIPPER THE VICTIMS:—

MARY ANN NICHOLLS

Polly Nicholls was proud of her new bonnet. The brown linsey frock, black rubbed wool stockings and two petticoats were a little the worse for wear but the black straw hat was new and Polly thought it might help her get the price of a doss for the night. She was a popular cheerful woman whose downfall in life had been the bottle. Her marriage to a printer's machinist had broken down because of her slovenly habits and she had lost contact with her five children and had not seen her husband for three years. If she could focus on the broken mirror she carried in her pocket she would not have been too impressed with her own reflection; at forty-two she looked much older and the gradual decline in her life from broken marriage to Lambeth workhouse, domestic service and prostitution had taken its toll. She had stolen £3 from her last job and probably spent it on gin, but tonight the 31st August, 1888 she was broke again and at 2.30 a.m. staggered away from the Frying Pan public house along Whitechapel Road to find her next and last customer . . . . Jack the Ripper.

Within an hour Polly was dead. Her body found lying on her back and skirt pushed up over her knees. A knife had been jabbed into the lower part of her abdomen and drawn upwards, not once but twice. The first cut veered to the right slitting up the groin and passing over the left hip.

The second cut went straight upward, along the centre of the body and reached the breast bone. She had effectively been ripped from the throat to her belly. Blood oozed from a horrendous gash in her throat which had been slashed twice from left to right, severing the windpipe and gullet. No part of the body, however, was taken away as was later to be the case.

Polly did not cry out or appear to have made any struggle and whether she saw her murderer we shall never know. Mary Ann Nicholls has the unfortunate distinction of becoming the first definite victim of the world's most notorious criminal.

43. Bucks Row.

44. Hanbury Street where Jack the Ripper and Annie Chapman passed.

DARK ANNIE

Annie Chapman was wandering the streets a week later for the same reason as Polly Nicholls: she had no money. Less than 5 ft. tall with wavy brown hair and a large thick nose, she liked drink but would only get drunk on a Saturday night. She often did crochet work and sold flowers but her main source of income was prostitution. Wearing a long black coat and skirt she hacked the streets of Whitechapel through the early hours of the morning after being turned out of a doss house at 2.00 a.m. She may have been thinking of her two estranged children or her dead husband or the man she had lived with a sieve maker. She was probably however, wondering where her next pennies were coming from as she set eyes on a possible customer . . . .

Her body was found at 29 Hanbury Street, the head almost severed from the body by two deep cuts. She was discovered once again flat on her back with her clothes disarranged. Her chin and jaw was bruised and face swollen, the tongue protruding from the mouth.

Her abdomen had been laid open and intestines severed and placed over her shoulder. The stomach had been torn open and this time the Ripper went further, removing the uterus and upper portions of the vagina and two thirds of the bladder—Annie Chapman had been disembowelled.

Her worldly possessions were neatly laid out in a row at her feet. These consisted of two brass rings a few pennies and two farthings. Annie Chapman was buried at Manor Park Cemetry, East London.

The Ripper had claimed victim number two and his attacks were becoming more outrageous.

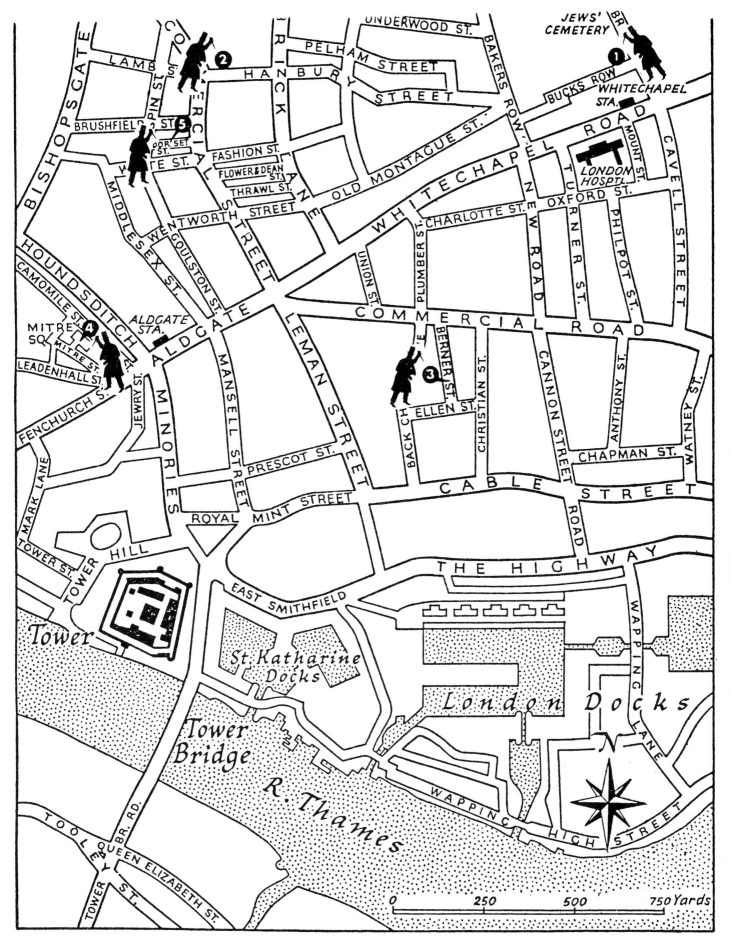

East London in 1888: Dates and Sites of Jack the Ripper's Murders

1. 31 August—Mary Ann Nicholls
2. 8 September—Annie Chapman
3. 30 September—Elizabeth Stride
4. 30 September—Catherine Eddowes
5. 9 November—Mary Jane Kelly

ELIZABETH STRIDE

Elizabeth Gustaafsdotter was born near Gothenburg, Sweden on 27th November, 1843 and died on 30th September, 1888 age 44. What exactly happened in her life prematurely cut short, is not certain as Long Liz (as she was to become known) had a certain amount of difficulty separating fact from fiction. She married a carpenter and supposedly lost her husband and two children on the Priness Alice disaster on the River Thames, though it has been hinted that she made up this story to conceal her separation. Lately she had been living with a labourer, Michael Kidney and earned her money by sewing and charring. To make up her wages she worked as a prostitute in the evening and after a meal of cheese and potatoes started her search for customers on that wet and windy night. She had a bunch of flowers pinned to her dress and wore a check silk scarf around her neck, though the pattern was soon to become unrecognizable.

Long Liz was found lying on her side in Berner Street, not on her back as were the first two victims, one hand pathetically clutching a packet of Cachous tissue paper. Her throat had been slit from left to right, the windpipe cut in two. She was bruised on the shoulders and chest but otherwise there were no other injuries or mutilations. It seems likely the Ripper was interrupted in his evil deed, and frustrated, looked for his fourth victim the same night.

CATHERINE EDDOWES

Catherine Eddowes was dressed for business; her dress dark green with a pattern of Michaelmas Daisies and Golden Lillies, was covered by a black cloth jacket with imitation fur collar and three large metal buttons. Under these outer garments she wore a thin white vest, drab linsey skirt and dark green alpaca petticoat with a white chemise and brown rubbed stockings, recently repaired. Her hat was the piece de resistance, the black straw bonnet being trimmed with black and green velvet and black beads. Round Catherine's neck was a piece of ribbon and cloth from an old white coarse apron.

She was just back from hop picking in Kent and at 43, probably found the work more exhausting than in her youth. The money earned had by now all been spent on drink and indeed, Catherine Eddowes, or Anne Kelly as she liked to be known, had pawned her companion's boots and flannel shirt to get some money for a bed for the night. The only bed she had found on the night of September 29th/30th was in the prison cell, after being arrested due to her drunkeness. She was released when she sobered up at about 12.30. Catherine had finished singing and after asking the time she was sent out into the night by the jailer at Bishopsgate police station. She went straight from the long arm of the law into those of a very disturbed and frustrated man, the blood still wet from an earlier victim.

Catherine was found lying on her back, legs apart, the face gashed and right eye damaged. Her lower eyelids had been nicked, and the lobe of her right ear along with part of her nose was missing. The intestines had been pulled out and laid across the right shoulder and it appeared that someone had frenziedly plunged his fist into her body and pulled out what he desired. The uterus and left kidney had been cut away and removed.

The local P.C. named Watkins said that he had been in the police force a long time but had 'never saw such a sight'. The body had been ripped open like a pig in the market.

Catherine Eddowes' worldly possessions were listed in the Times and help us imagine the lives thousands of women lived just a hundred years ago. She carried a piece of string, a white handkerchief, a blunt table knife, a matchbox containing cotton, two clay pipes, a red cigarette case, five pieces of soap, a small box with tea and sugar, a portion of a pair of spectacles, a small comb, a red mitten and a ball of worsted.

The remains were placed in a polished elm coffin and interred in Ilford Cemetery witnessed by 500 people, a posse of reporters and a large police presence.

Catherine Eddowes had become the fourth victim of the man soon to become the notorious Jack the Ripper.

45. Mitre Square, where Catherine Eddowes met her death.

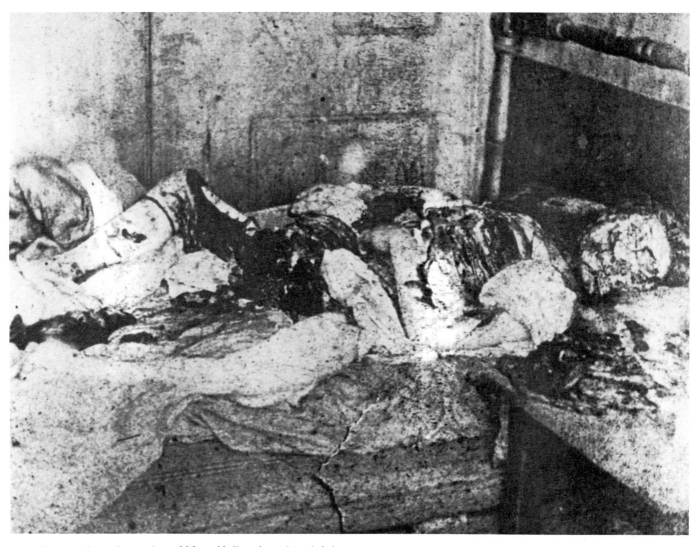

46. The butchered remains of Mary Kelly, almost certainly
the Ripper's last victim.

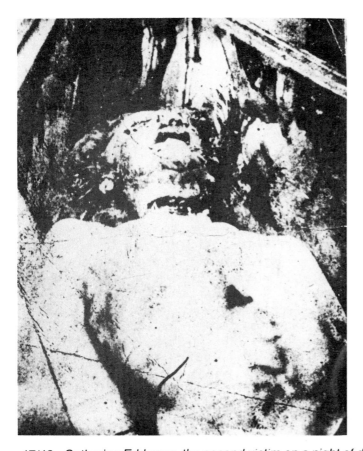

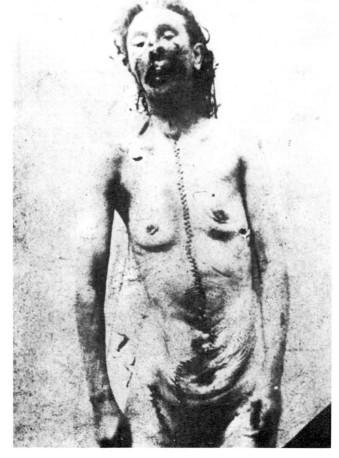

47/48. Catherine Eddowes, the second victim on a night of double-murder.

MARY KELLY

Mary had been in London for five years and at twenty-five was still attractive, despite the difficult life she had experienced. She was worried about the thirty-five shillings owed in rent and was determined to earn the money in practically the only way she knew how, on the street.

Mary was born in Limerick and taken with her six brothers and one sister to Wales where her father was employed at the steelworks. Mary herself married a collier at the age of sixteen and she seemed set for a life in the valleys when the first disaster in her life struck. She was informed that her husband had been killed in an explosion. From here on her life story is a little vague but it appears she spent some time with a 'client' in Paris before starting on the downward path to drink and prostitution in the East End.

On 8th November Mary went out along Commercial Street popping in at a few pubs for a quick nip of her favourite tipple—London Gin.

Anyone seeing her for the first time could be forgiven for staring, as she retained her fresh coloured Irish complexion and with a fine head of hair stretching down to her waist was a very attractive woman. She lived in fear of no one, having learned her trade in the Tiger Bay area of Cardiff and now had her pitch outside the Ten Bells pub in Commercial Street. (Ironically this is now known as "The Jack the Ripper"). What exactly happened to 'Black Mary' we shall never know but in the early hours of the morning, in her own room, she met her death and we can only hope it was a speedy exit.

Perhaps because this was the only Ripper murder perpetrated indoors, he having more time to set about his dissection, this was without a doubt the most gruesome

51. *This was Mary Kelly's local though then known as The Ten Bells. It was renamed by the landlady in the 1930's, a certain Annie Chapman.*

and bloodthirsty crime. Mary was found on the edge of the bed nearest the door wearing just the remains of a chemise. The body was not ripped apart but sliced up, as if the murderer was a butcher preparing trays of meat for the shop window. On the mattress in the sparsely furnished room lay a mass of raw flesh, the thighs down to the feet and the forehead having been skinned. Her throat had been cut from ear to ear and the head was attached to the rest of the body only by a thin layer of skin. The nose and breasts had been cut off and were placed on the table by the side of the bed. The liver, heart and kidneys were removed and one of the dead woman's hands had been pushed into her stomach. The left arm, like the head was attached to the body by skin only.

Mary's face was completely destroyed and pieces of flesh dripped from the picture rails. Several small parcels containing parts of the body were wrapped up and sent to the mortuary and it took about six hours to assemble the body into some resemblance of a human being. Mary Kelly was three months pregnant.

BLIND-MAN'S BUFF.

(As played by the Police.)

"TURN ROUND THREE TIMES,
AND CATCH WHOM YOU MAY!"

52. *Cartoon from Punch, mocking the police attempts at catching The Ripper.*

THE HUNT FOR JACK THE RIPPER

"I am down on whores and shan't quit ripping them till I do get buckled"

53. *An imposing view of Scotland Yard.*

The police were in an unenviable position. The five murders seemed motiveless; no witnesses saw the killings; nobody heard a scream. Medical experts were arguing with each other and the perpetrator of the crimes seemed to vanish into thin air after each slaughtering leaving very little in the way of clues.

The problems faced by the police were manifold. Without the help of scientific methods employed in murder cases today they were faced with a hysterical public, anxious politicians and questions from the Queen herself. The Ripper was not only to affect the lives of prostitutes in the East End but also, single-handedly as it were, the careers of several prominent figures. George Bernard Shaw was an emerging young socialist at the time of the murders and he noted in a letter to the Star that;

> 'Whilst we conventional Social Democrats were wasting our time on education, agitation and organisation, some independent genius had taken the matter in hand, and by simply murdering and disembowelling four women, converted the proprietry press to an inept form of communism'.

On the previous pages we have had a taste of the conditions in the East End. Reports of women beaten or kicked to death, jumped on till they were crushed, chopped, stabbed or deliberately set alight were far from being uncommon, the assailants rarely being brought to justice. The discovery of a body therefore on the night of 31st August 1888 did not unduly alarm the local population, even though it was the third murder that year of a prostitute within an area of three hundred yards.

Polly Nicholls was found in Bucks Row by a market porter who was joined a little later by a policeman. On a perfunctory examination of the body he came to the conclusion that the deceased had committed suicide by cutting her own throat! The investigations from the start were carried out in a very slipshod manner and it was not even discovered that Polly Nicholls had been dis-emboweled until three and a half hours after the discovery of her body. So much for the suicide theory! To add to the general lack of professionalism shown by the police, Inspector John Spratting stood by whilst two workhouse inmates removed the clothes and washed the corpse!

The surgeon who examined the body thought that a hand had been held across the mouth (bruising showed this to be the right hand) and the wounds made, probably with a knife, from left to right. Evidence seemed to be pointing towards the likelyhood of the attacker being left-handed. When the extent of the injuries became known the press started to show an interest and reported that the foreman of the jury at the inquest offered a reward of twenty-five pounds for information leading to the arrest of the murderer.

48

Maybe it was because the murder took place near a slaughterhouse and could have been caused by a corkcutter or shoemaker's knife that police started an intensive search for 'Leather Apron'; a man wearing this apparel was reported to have mistreated prostitutes in the East End.

With the discovery of the second body just a week or so later at 29 Hanbury Street, the public and press and even the police came to the realisation that there was some kind of homicidal maniac on the loose. All manner of stories began to circulate by word of mouth in the densely populated suburbs. One claimed that the killer had scrawled on the wall 'Five — 15 more and I will give myself up'.

The public knew the murderer as Leather Apron (the name of Jack the Ripper had not yet been coined) and the newspapers referred to the crimes as the Whitechapel Murders. Police had begun investigations in over two hundred doss-houses looking for the mysterious Leather Apron. They were very vague as to what exactly they were seeking, but the day after the Chapman murder fourteen suspects were arrested and later released and the first description of the Ripper was circulated, though its source is not known.

Age 37, Height 5 ft. 7 ins.; rather dark beard and moustache. Dress; shirt, dark jacket, dark vest and trousers, black scarf and black felt hat. Spoke with a foreign accent.

The police were for some reason convinced it was a foreigner and there was a great deal of resentment against the thousands of immigrants who had settled in the area. The Leather Apron theory was compounded when a scrubbed leather apron was found in the backyard of Hanbury Square. All police investigations were centred on the immigrant population with the chief suspects being butchers, slaughtermen and craftsmen—and several attacks on this class of person were reported. The idea of an Englishman or a 'Gentleman' being in any way responsible did not seem to have occurred to the police at this stage of their investigation.

The public were pressing the police for an arrest and on the 10th September it was announced that Leather Apron had been arrested! He was named as Joseph Pizer, a Polish Jew employed as a shoemaker. The only evidence against him seems to have been that he possessed a number of long-bladed knives and it was noticed that children used to follow him in the street shouting out 'Leather Apron yah'. Some members of the press needed little more evidence than this however and he was described as having 'grizzly black strips of hair and a cruel sardonic look'.

Pizer was found however to have a cast-iron alibi and went from the coroners courts to the civil court to bring libel actions against the newspapers. The police were becoming frustrated and desperate and detectives disguised themselves as butchers, but all to no avail and the theory of Leather Apron began to loose credibility. More and more weird schemes were proposed by newspapers and individuals in order to catch the monster, Amongst the proposals were;

(1) Prostitutes should walk in pairs.
(2) All prostitutes should be given whistles.
(3) Scotland Yard should disguise men as women.

(4) Young clean-shaven boxers should be disguised as women with steel collars attached to their necks (there were no policewomen at this time).

At the second inquest, that of Annie Chapman, greater care was taken with the body with two nurses in attendance. The coroner said that the murder weapon was probably a very sharp knife and also thought that there was some anatomical skill in the dissection of the body. The courtroom was cleared of women and boys during the testimony and The Times thought the details of the mutilation were totally unfit for publication.

The eyes of Annie Chapman were photographed by the police as it was a popular belief that when a person died their last view of life, in this case probably Jack the Ripper, was indelibly printed on the pupils. Needless to say this line of enquiry did not greatly help the police in their hunt.

The Daily Telegraph of the time helped focus attention on the plight of the poor in the East End:

'Dark Annie's spirit still walks Whitechapel, unavenged by Justice . . . . And yet even this forlorn, despised citizeness of London cannot be said to have suffered in vain. On the contrary, she has effected more by her death than many long speeches in Parliament and countless columns of letters to the newspapers could have brought about.

She has forced innumerable people who never gave a serious thought to the subject before, to realize how it is, and where it is, that our vast floating population—the waifs and strays of our thoroughfares—live and sleep at night and what sort of accommodation our rich and enlightened capital provides for them, after so many Acts of Parliament passed to improve the dwellings of the poor, and so many millions spent by our Board of Works, our vestries . . . . . 'Dark Annie' will effect in one way what fifty Secretraries of State could never accomplish . . . .''

Flower and Dean Street, Spitalfields.

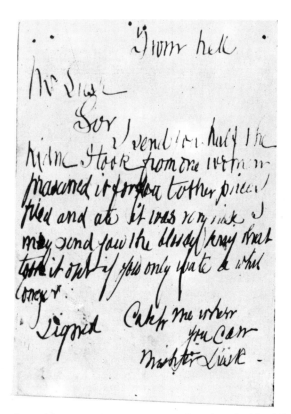

55. One of the many letters supposedly written by The Ripper

Everyone and anyone had their own theory as to the motive behind the two murders and after the removal of certain organs from Annie Chapman it was suggested she'd been butchered in order to remove and sell parts of her body, even fresher than the specimens obtained by Burke and Hare. An American had enquired at medical schools as to the availability of the organs that were later found missing and he was offering £20 per sample. He intended to preserve the organs in glycerine so they would be in a flaccid condition. The medical profession were incensed by this slur and protested vigorously until the police dropped this line of enquiry.

The police were becoming more and more frustrated and made several arrests on very slender evidence, usually drunkards telling prostitutes they were the murderer and threatening to carve them up 'in the Whitechapel Manner!'. Several of those arrested were eventually despatched to the lunatic asylum. The police however, were no nearer finding the identity of the true killer and the press started attacking those in charge of the hunt and mocking them in cartoons. The main butt of their anger was the Chief of the Metropolitan Police, Sir Charles Warren. He was a handsome moustached man who wore a monocle but his appointment had been made more for his potential to keep the public from rebelling than his ability to solve crime. He had very little experience of police work having been a General in the British Army in Egypt before returning to take up the prestigious police post. Most writers on the murders claim that Sir Charles Warren was completely inept and ill-suited to his job. At least one recent investigator into the murders however believes that the Chief of the Metropolitan Police was involved in a deliberate cover-up which, if revealed, would have made the Watergate scandal appear of trifling importance in comparison.

The local people were not content to just sit back and wait for another murder and so volunteers were organised to assist the police in nightly patrols. Many lone wolves operated, probably the most famous being Dr. Wimslow who had specialised in the criminally insane and he was often to be seen sporting his full set of mutton-chop whiskers amongst the prostitutes of Whitechapel, his own theory being that the Ripper was a religious maniac. One director of the Bank of England dressed as a navvy, scoured the streets carrying a pick-axe in the hope of catching the Ripper.

There were of course many letters written by people claiming they were the Ripper and two days before the double murder of Elizabeth Stride and Catherine Eddowes the Central News Agency of Fleet Street received the following letter written in red ink and postmarked 'London East Central'.

Dear Boss,
I keep on hearing the police have caught me, but they won't fix me just yet. I have laughed when they look so clever and talk about being on the right track. The joke about Leather Apron gave me real fits.

I am down on whores and I shan't quit ripping them till I do get buckled. Grand work, the last job was. I gave the lady no time to squeal. How can they catch me now? I love my work and want to start again. You will soon hear of me and my funny little games.

I saved some of the proper red stuff in a ginger beer bottle over the last job, to write with, but it went a little thick like glue and I can't use it. Red ink is fit enough, I hope. Ha! Ha!

The next job I do I shall clip the lady's ears off and send them to the police, just for jolly, wouldn't you? Keep this letter back until I do a bit more work, then give it out straight. My knif's so nice and sharp, I want to get to work right away if I get the chance. Good luck,
                Yours truly,
              JACK THE RIPPER

Don't mind me giving the trade name. Wasn't good enough to post this before I got all the red ink off my hands; curse it. No luck yet. They say I am a doctor now. Ha! Ha!

The letter contained many Americanisms and was followed by a postcard with a large bloody thumbprint saying that there was going to be a double-event.
The postcard said;

'I was not codding dear old Boss when I gave you the tip. You'll hear about saucy Jack's work tomorrow double event this time number one squealed a bit couldn't finish straight off. Had no time to get ears for police thanks for keeping last letter back till I got to work again.'

It was mailed on Sunday the 13th October, after the double murder but before the information was released to the press. Whether these communications were written by the Ripper or not, from that day on the name was to stick.

Two bodies were found on the night of 29th/30th September, the first that of Elizabeth Stride, being discovered in Berner Street and the second Catherine Eddowes, some ten minutes walk away in Mitre Square. The culprit certainly had an excellent knowledge of the area and was a fast worker, Mitre Street being patrolled every fifteen minutes.

_55a._

POLICE THE ILLUSTRATED NEWS

LAW COURTS and WEEKLY RECORD

No. 1,292.   SATURDAY, NOVEMBER 17, 1888.   Price One Penny.

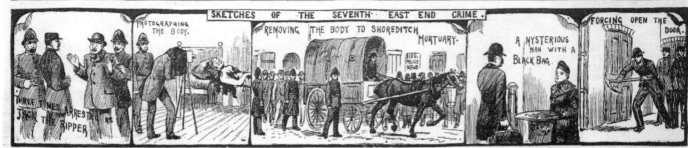

SKETCHES OF THE SEVENTH EAST END CRIME.

THE SEVENTH HORRIBLE MURDER BY THE MONSTER OF THE EAST-END.

THE SEVENTH VICTIM!
PICKED OUT FOR SLAUGHTER BY THE EAST-END FIEND.
FROM DESCRIPTIONS GIVEN BY HER INTIMATE FRIENDS.

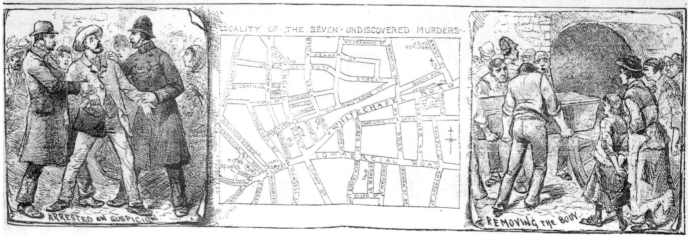

LOCALITY OF THE SEVEN UNDISCOVERED MURDERS.

55b.

Probably the most remarkable and unexplained factor in the killings was that the murderer seemed to be invisible and hunted so stealthily that hardly a sound was heard. A woman who lived just a few yards away from where the body of victim number two was discovered said she could not sleep that night, but never heard a sound.

The killer it seems was crying out to be noticed after his crimes and the one clue which has baffled Ripperologists for decades was the discovery of the first real clue in Goulston Street at 2.55 on the night of the double murder. A police constable noticed a piece of Catherine Eddowes apron lying on the ground, which had been hacked off with a kinfe. It had not been there when he had passed at 2.20. More importantly however he noticed chalked on the black dado of a wall above the apron, a message written in a round schoolboy hand;

"The Juwes are the men that will not be blamed for nothing".

He searched the area but found nothing and reported the writing on the wall to Commercial Street Police Station. What then happened is probably one of the biggest blunders in police history. Sir Charles Warren went to the scene of the writing and ordered it to be removed before any photographs could be taken. His reason for this action he argued was that the writing would prove of great offence to the Jewish population. Other high ranking police officers were furious at his actions and many Ripperologists feel he had ulterior motives and must have been protecting someone of very high stature.

The double murder brought panic to the East End, the local inhabitants losing confidence in the police and 4,000 women of Whitechapel wrote a petition to Queen Victoria who later replied that she was graciously pleased to see the petition.

Just over two weeks after the double murder, a parcel was received by a Mr. George Lusk, Chairman of the Whitechapel Vigilance Committee and one of the most devoted Ripper hunters. Opening the cardboard box he found a portion of kidney with a letter enclosed. It read:—

"From hell, Mr. Lusk, sor, I send you half the kidne I took from one woman prasarved it for you, tother piece I fried and ate it, was ver nise I may send you the bloody knif that took it out if you only wate a while longer. Catch me when you can Mishter Lusk".

The kidney was examined and found to be of human origin and had been placed in spirits within a few hours of its removal. It was a 'ginny' kidney which meant that it had belonged to a heavy drinker—certainly not uncommon in those days. It was said to belong to a woman aged about forty-five and had been removed within the last three weeks. It could of course have been sent by a medical student as a prank but there was a strong possibility that it had once belonged to Catherine Eddowes. The renal artery is three inches long, two inches were found left in Eddowes' body and the renal artery in the portion of kidney sent to Mr. Lusk was one inch long. Furthermore, the kidney left in the corpse was in an advanced state of Brights disease, as was the portion of the kidney sent in the cardboard box!

In the six weeks between murders four and five—the Rippers last and most horrifying—the police received nearly 1,500 letters, some from cranks, others professing to be the Ripper but the majority suggesting ways in which he may be caught. The police were no longer making arrests for fear of being mocked by the press and it was this press—in the form of the Times—which was indirectly responsible for perhaps the most far-fetched plan to capture the mystery assailant. They pointed out in an article that twelve years before in Blackburn, Lancs. a murderer had been caught after bloodhounds had been used to track him. Sir Charles Warren was now a desperate man under intense pressure and he decided to contact the dog handler a Mr. Brough. He was summoned to London with his two bloodhounds, Barnaby and Burgho and in trials to prove their effectiveness, Warren himself acted as the prey, being successfully tracked down by the bloodhounds in a London park. The trials were not exactly conclusive but were enough for Warren to insist that if the murderer struck again, nothing was to be moved until the bloodhounds arrived. Imagine this, in one of the most densely populated areas in the world!

The strain was beginning to tell on Warren and he resigned just before the murder of Mary Kelly. She was almost certainly the killer's last victim and many writers feel that because this murder was so different from the others, and without a doubt the most sadistic, there are more clues to the killer's identity to be obtained from this homicide than any of the other four. Mary Kelly was not one of the many haggard middle-aged prostitutes to be found in Whitechapel but still in the prime of life. She was not murdered and quickly disemboweled in the street, but systematically cut up indoors over what must have been a lengthy period. Was the killer's bloodlust finally satisfied? Had he finally become unhinged? The attitude of the police in the weeks after the discovery of the body seemed to give the impression, many officers believed the killer had committed suicide.

Mary Kelly's body was discoverd at no. 13 Millers Court, but nobody was allowed into the house until the bloodhounds had had a sniff around. But the bloodhounds had been returned to their owner, and precious hours were lost trying to trace their whereabcuts.

The Queen who showed much more interest in the murders than the conditions of the mass of her subjects, wrote a letter from Balmoral Castle to the Prime Minister the Marquis of Salisbury:—

"This new ghastly murder shows the absolute necessity for some very decided action. All three courts must be lit and our detectives improved. They are not what they should be".

The murders ceased almost as suddenly as they had begun. The autumn of terror had lasted three months, the mystery—100 years.

55a/55b. The public's interest in the murders was fuelled by the imaginative art work in the Illustrated Police News of the day.

56. Who is Jack the Ripper?

THE SUSPECTS

Several theories as to the identity of the Ripper have been put forward over the decades. They range from the ridiculous—a Canadian wearing Snow Shoes—to the Royal Family,—Queen Victoria's Grandson, the Duke of Clarence.

Six out of seven police officers at the time of the murders believed this assailant to be a foreign doctor or butcher and Sir Charles Warren, head of the investigation, thought the murderer was a sex maniac who committed suicide after the disembowelling of Mary Kelly.

Sir Melville Macnaghten former Chief of the C.I.D. was also convinced that the murderer committed suicide on or about the 10th November. He was adamant that the Ripper only murdered five people, saying:—

> "The Whitechapel murderer had five victims and five victims only"

When it was suggested that the Ripper committed a murder two years later he wrote:—

> "It will be noticed that the fury of the mutilations increased in each case, and seemingly, the appetite only became sharpened by indulgence. It seems then, highly improbable that the murderer would have suddenly stopped in November '88, and been content to recommence operations by merely prodding a girl behind some 2 years and 4 months afterwards. A much more rational theory is that the murderer's brain gave way altogether after his awful glut in Miller's Court, and that he immediately committed suicide, or, as a possible alternative, was found to be hopelessly mad by his relations, that he was confined by them in some asylum.".

Sir Melville went on to name three suspects who we shall investiigate briefly, along with some more modern theories.

Britain's most famous detective, Sherlock Holmes was 'alive' during the horrific murders. What did he make of them? Sir Arthur Conan Doyle's son Adrian summed up his father's thoughts on the case.

> "He considered it likely that the man had a rough knowledge of surgery and probably clothed himself as a woman to avoid undue attention by the police and to approach his victims without arousing suspicion on their part"

The idea of a man being dressed in womens' clothing or indeed a woman herself being responsible are given extra credence when we consider the facts that a burnt set of female clothes were found in Mary Kelly's flat. In 1938 William Stewart put forward a theory that the killer was indeed a murderess—a midwife, Jill the Ripper; this explaining the knowledge of anatomy. It has also been stated that Mary Kelly, like many prostitutes, had lesbian tendencies and the killing may have been one of revenge.

Over the years however, four or five men have become the main suspects and if one was a betting man the favourite would probably be Montague J. Druitt.

57. Sir Arthur Conan Doyle (Below). Thought Jack the Ripper dressed as a woman.

MONTAGUE J. DRUITT

Born 15th august, 1857. He studied classics and may have studied medicine for a year before switching to Law and being called to the bar in 1885. He worked as a barrister and a teacher on Blackheath before being sacked on 1st December, 1888, approximately one month after the last murder. He was last seen alive two days later when he wrote:—

"Since Friday I felt I was going to be like Mother [she had become insane] and the best thing for me was to die."

He filled the pockets of his overcoat with stones and threw himself into the Thames, he was 31 years old.

Why was the man a leading suspect? It seems that Druitt had a cruel and sexual aura, and he feared for his own sanity. His dismissal from his teaching job and subsequent suicide came just after the last murder and from that time they, of course, ceased. Indeed his own family thought him guilty and he was also left-handed.

The main evidence against him however, is rather circumstantial. He had no alibi at the time of the killings. He was a keen cricketer and for many years had played for Blackheath (South London) and also for teams in his native Dorset. The day after Mary Ann Nicholls was murdered (about 3.30 a.m. on Friday, 31st August) Druitt played cricket in Dorset and 5 hours after the murder of Annie Chapman, Druitt was playing cricket again—this time for Blackheath. His whereabouts on the other nights is unknown.

For reasons we may still not know today, after Druitt's suicide the police closed their file on the case and—coincidentally or not—the murders ceased!

58. Montague Druitt. Drowned himself in the Thames shortly after the last murder.

DR.STANLEY

The first full length book about the murders points the finger of guilt at a Dr. Stanley a Harley Street surgeon whose son died of syphilis contracted from the high class prostitute Mary Kelly.

NEILL CREAM—(even though he was probably in prison at the time of the murders).

A small American, Neill Cream is still considered a suspect because of his famous last words. After being sent to the gallows for the murder of a prostitute Matilda Clover and several other women in 1892 Cream cried out as the trapdoor dropped:—

"I'm Jack the . . . . . ."

The end of the sentence was cut short.

KOMINSKI

A Polish Jew and resident of Whitechapel, he was one of Sir Melville Macnaghten's three suspects. He wrote of him:—

"This man became insane owing to many years indulgence in solitary vices. He had a great hatred of women, especially of the prostitute class, and had strong homicidal tendencies: He was removed to a lunatic asylum about March 1889. There were many crimes connected with this man which made him a strong 'suspect'.

MICHAEL OSTROG

He was Macnaghten's third suspect and he describes him as:—

"A Russian doctor, and a convict, who was frequently detained in a lunatic asylum as a homicidal maniac. This man's antecedents were of the worst possible type, and his whereabouts at the time of the murders could never be ascertained".

DR. ALEXANDER PEDACHENKO

Another 'front runner' in the Ripper stakes must be a most enigmatic Russian. Dr. Alexander Pedachenko. He was a Russian criminal lunatic apparently sent to London by the Tsar's secret police in order to embarrass the English police. He had many aliases and had been trained as a barber surgeon (it might be an appropriate place to add here that the technique of surgery in Britain and the rest of Europe at the time differed greatly due to the use of anaesthetics in the British Isles—it is thought the bodies were cut up in the European way). Pedachenko returned to Russia and died in an asylum—after he had been detained by the police following the murder of a woman in St. Petersburg.

The Ochrana Gazette, official bulletin of the Russian Secret Police, named him as the man wanted for the murder of five women in East London. Sir Basil Thomson, former Assistant Commissioner of the Metropolitan Police said that the belief of the C.I.D. officers was that the work of that Russian doctor, Pedachenko seemed to fit the bill.

THE DUKE OF CLARENCE

Queen Victoria's Grandson, who reputedly used to leave the palace in disguise to go and mix with the locals in the East end. He was caught by the police in a raid at a homosexual brothel in Cleveland Street and died of influenza four years after the final murder. It is tenuously stated that Prince Eddie may have learned dissecting skills through cutting up animals after hunting and from the operations he used to watch.

Suspicion seems to have fallen on Prince Eddie largely because of the great interest shown in the case by his grandmother Queen Victoria.

J. K. STEPHEN

Stephen was the Duke of Clarence's lover and had a paranoic hatred of women which may be seen in his poem, Ten little whores of Jerusalem.

SIR WILLIAM GULL

One of the recent big sellers about the identity of Jack the Ripper suggests that William Gull, the Royal Physician himself carried out the murders, picking up the prostitutes in a carriage and slitting their throats there before dumping them, thus explaining the lack of blood.

It is stated that his motive was to protect Prince Eddie who was supposed to have made a Catholic woman pregnant during one of his sorties and Mary Kelly and possibly the other victims had found out about this and were going to either blackmail or reveal all. The country was going through troubled times and the thought of a Catholic Heir to the throne could have sparked off serious civil disturbances.

. . . .

These are just some of the suspects; others include a Texan Vivisectionist, a policeman, an excitable medical student, a cannibal, a Malay, a Russian, a Frenchman, an epileptic medical student, Ameer Ben Ali, a female abortionist with a male accomplice, a Norweigan sailor, a Doctor merchant, a woman revenging the death of her prostitute sister and a Canadian wearing snow shoes.

One cannot help but be amazed at the xenophobic bias in the list of suspects. One thing is for sure however, we haven't heard the last of Jack the Ripper.

59. Prince Eddie. The Duke of Clarence was often found in uncompromising positions in the East End.

BEDLAM
AND THE STORY OF HANNA SNELL

'It was so loathesomely and filthily kept that it was not fit for any man to come into . . . (1598).'

Situated variously in Bishopsgate, Moorfields and Lambeth, one of the main attractions over the centuries for the London mob was the Bethlehem Royal Hospital or 'Bedlam'. So famous has the hospital become that the word has been accepted into the English language signifying 'a scene of wild uproar'.

The lunatic asylum made a lot of money from the public up to the year 1770, as visitors were admitted to see the lunatics as we might visit the zoo today, the entrance fee being 1d. In a report to the House of Commons in 1815 Dr. Connoly reported that he found in one of the side-rooms;

> "about ten patients each chained by one arm or leg to the wall, each wearing a sort of dressing gown with nothing to fasten it. Some sensible and accomplished, some imbeciles. Many women were locked up naked with only one blanket."

One inmate was chained to her bed for eight years, the matron feeling the prisoner would murder her if released. When finally the date of her release arrived she became tranquil, nursing two dolls which she imagined were her children. Another patient, well-known to the many visitors, wore a straw cap and promised to declare war on the stars if rewarded with a bottle of wine. One of the most famous patients, often visited by members of Parliament was a certain William Norris. For twelve years he was chained with a strong iron ring round his neck. His arms were pinioned by an iron bar and he could only move twelve feet away from the wall. In this position he lived as normal a life as possible before dying shortly after his release. Two more patients spent a total of over eighty years between them in Bedlam for trying to kill the same man. James Hadfield was confined for 39 years for attempting to shoot George III. He spent his time writing verses on the deaths of his cats and birds, his only companions in the hospital. Margaret Nicholson spent 42 years in solitary confinement for attempting to stab the same King.

William Cooper described his thoughts on visiting the asylum as a youngster;

> "The madness of some of them has such a humorous air, and displayed itself in so many whimsical freaks, that it was impossible not to be entertained at the same time that I was angry with myself for being so."

The life stories of some of the patients who finished their days in Bedlam make fascinating reading, I have chosen just one as a means of illustration, the story of Hanna Snell: As a young girl some two hundred years ago, Hanna fell for the charms of a Dutch sailor, their romance eventually leading to marriage. But the relationship became strained when he became disenchanted and started visiting the local prostitutes. He went back to sea, having left her short

59a. William Norris in Bedlam.

of money and with a baby which later died. Hanna, not the kind of girl to feel sorry for herself and with typical East End resourcefulness, decided to seek out the husband who she still professed to love. So dressed as a man she enlisted, first as a soldier and later as a marine and was sent to the East Indies and experienced many perilous adventures. On her way back from India she heard by chance that her husband had been executed for murder.

With her identity still undiscovered Hanna returned to Wapping. Later a sailor discovered her sex and once exposed she was offered several proposals of marriage. Declining them all she started a career on the stage appearing as a sailor—and both in her professional and private life she continued to wear men's clothing. Later in life she set up a pub, the sign outside painted on one face with a jolly British Tar and on the other a Marine. The name was inscribed underneath: 'The Widow in Masquerade' or 'The Female Warrior'. Late in life Hanna married and had another son but unfortunately became insane and for the last few years of her life had to endure the atrocious conditions in Bedlam.

The last site of the hospital in London is now 'The Imperial War Museum' and its present location in Kent.

WOOLWICH
HIGHWAYMEN AND BOMBS

There have been two main lines of communication between London and Europe since Roman times, the River Thames and the Old Dover Road. About eight miles from the city the road rises to 446 ft. at Shooters Hill (so called because archers used to see the range they could get from the top of the hill), this being 5 ft. 1 in. higher than St. Paul's Cathedral. Henry VIII spent a great deal of his time in South-East London and at Shooters Hill met two hundred archers, one impersonating Robin Hood, who he joined in a days sport, finishing the day with a meal of venison and wine. The area is still wooded as it was in the days when it became a notorious haunt for highwaymen. The road was steep and narrow and being closed in by thick woods made for an easy escape. Highwaymen would stop coaches or indeed any travellers and ask the the now famous question:

'Your money or your life, stand and deliver'.

The famous Dick Turpin had connections with the area though worked mostly on the other side of the Thames. If any of these highway robbers were ever caught they were executed and their bodies left hanging from a gibbet on the road as a warning to others and it was not uncommon to see and indeed smell several bodies hanging by the road. The diarist Samuel Pepys wrote in 1661

"Mrs Anne and I rode under the man that hangs upon Shooters Hill and a filthy sight it was to see how his flesh is shrunk to his bones".

There are two ghosts, both female, who have been witnessed near the bottom of Shooters Hill. Beware on misty autumn evenings as you may see a mysterious lady dressed in dark clothes who hanged herself from an elm tree on the road after her married lover failed to keep an appointment one night. Another unknown ghost haunts the crossroads with Well Hall Road, wandering around screaming in terror and despair after having been fatally wounded by a savage gashing to the back of her neck.

61. *George Webb & Richard Russell at the place of execution on Shooters Hill.*

On Tuesday evening two persons were attacked on Blackheath, by a single highwayman, who demanded their money, but said he wanted no rings or watches. They gave him two guineas and some silver, but one of the persons asked him for a shilling to pay the turnpike to London; he by mistake returned one of the guineas. He afterwards committed another robbery in the sight of many people, it being the time of Blackheath fair.

60. *A warning to travellers.*

62. The 'Great Harry' built at Woolwich and part of the 'woode wall of England'.

Woolwich has long been a garrison town and famous for the manufacture of armaments in the arsenal. Indeed it is the original home of the famous Arsenal Football Club (now in North London) and also where the somewhat idiocyncratic English licensing laws still waiting to be updated were introduced during the first World War. (During the war the arsenal workers would go to the pub at lunchtime—and stay there. Production could not keep up with demand so a law was introduced governing the times that pubs should open and close).

The garrison building on Woolwich Common (built between 1776 and 1802) is in the Guinness book of records as the longest Georgian facade. Woolwich was also one of the major dockyards building ships to provide 'the woode walls of England', the home fleet which kept Britain safe from invasion. The Great Harry was built here in an area that once consisted of over fifty-six acres with a frontage of 3680ft. The shipyard was closed and moved to Chatham in 1869 as the water was too shallow, the boats having to go downstream before being fitted with guns. Woolwich cemetery contains one hundred and twenty bodies of those who drowned just downriver on The Princess Alice on 3rd September 1878.

Woolwich has always been home to many young soldiers and this is why it was singled out in 1974 for an attack that so shocked the local inhabitants, including myself, that they will never forget the day of destruction. For several years the British public had been used to reading about the troubles and bombings in Northern Ireland but in 1973 the dispute was brought to the heart of London with the I.R.A. planting a bomb in a car outside The Old Bailey. The car disintegrated, resulting in over 200 casualties mostly caused by flying glass, some of which was driven into the concrete and can still be seen. There had been a warning and nineteen courts were evacuated although two police officers were badly injured. The bombings had come to London! But not only had they come to London—they had also come to Woolwich.

A year later, on 7th November 1974, a bomb weighing between five and ten pounds and packed with long nails was lobbed through the window of the Kings Arms on Woolwich Common. The code word was 'bastards', a word that must have been going through the minds of those unfortunate customers inside. A part-time barman and soldier were killed and many others mutilated, bodies lying in pools of blood outside. The pub was chosen as it was a regular haunt of the young soldiers stationed just opposite. Being so late in the evening and on a Thursday (pay day) it was a miracle there was not a far greater loss of life. Luckily, some of the locals were playing cribbage in another pub and there was a disco in the barracks at the time. But the soldiers had been forewarned that this kind of attack might take place and had been instructed not to congregate in the one pub. Amazingly two children in bed upstairs slept through the whole bombing.

63. *The Georgian facade of Woolwich Garrison.*

64. *The King's Arms: The bomb was thrown through the window.*

65. Haunted by a ghost cited for rape!

CHARLTON HOUSE

Being somewhat off the tourist route, Charlton House is not visited as often as its splendid architecture and upkeep would merit. Built as a house for a Prince, it is without doubt one of the finest specimens of Jacobean architecture in the country. The Orangery, now a public lavatory, is thought to be the work of Inigo Jones, but the architect of the building, finished in 1612, is unknown.

The house is certainly worth an extended visit as it is of interest in more than an architectural sense. It was bought by a certain William Langhorn as an asylum for his old age after several years as governor of Madras, India. His greatest sorrow in life was that despite the two marriages, both late in life he was unable to produce an heir to his fortune when he died at the ripe old age of 85. It is said that Langhorne's ghost chases young girls around the house, and has even been accused of rape.

There is a spot on the landing, formerly overlooked by a carved devil's head, where visitors complained of a sudden chill. Two warders have also noticed this cold draught and one of their dogs always became agitated at the same spot on the landing.

During the first world war Charlton House was used as a Military Hospital, Lady Wilson, who was running the house at that time, warned the nurses not to put wounded soldiers in what was her bedroom. This warning was ignored and some men reported having seen a ghost. Indeed many overnight guests have complained of presences in their bedrooms and for a long time the house was closed at 10 p.m.

Langhorne may not be the only resident of Charlton House as a servant girl carrying a baby has been seen in the grounds. Whether this is a kind of taunt to the heirless Langhorne we shall probably never know. At whatever time of year, and whatever time of day your visit, you will feel a chill reception on the stairs of this haunted house.

66. Sir William Langhorne

61

67. From back to front: The Royal Observatory,
The Queen Anne House and The Royal
Naval College.

68. Greenwich Planetarium.

69. Pedestrian tunnel at Greenwich.

GREENWICH

As we pass through the Blackwall Tunnel to South London and Greenwich we have a shift in emphasis from the tragical to the historical. Not that South London did not have its seamier side, as we shall see. It is just overshadowed by the amount of history still on view here and Greenwich is highly recommended for a future return visit. We cannot do it justice on our short stay.

71. East meets West and time means nothing in Greenwich.

Greenwich, whose name is probably derived from Green Village, has within its boundaries one of the finest collections of beautiful historic buildings in the United Kingdom: The National Maritime Museum, including the Queen's House; Royal Naval College; Charlton House; Tudor Barn; Eltham Palace; Royal Academy and Sevendroog Castle. It also houses one of the oldest Royal Parks and the Royal Observatory, where the Meridian Line splits the world into East and West. The park has an extremely interesting history of its own.

70. The Blackwall Tunnel. Home of the phantom hitch-hiker.

Back to the Tunnel. Many lives were lost during the boring work in the last century, but the ghost who has been seen here is a far more contemporary figure. He can be seen in full leather gear and helmet as he has not been able to leave since 1972, when he died in a motor cycle accident. Keep your eye out for phantom hitch hikers too. This story originates from the same year as the motor cycle accident and once again concerns this form of transport. In 1972 a motor cyclist stopped to pick up a young male thumbing a lift. The conversation coming through the tunnel had to be shouted because of the noise of traffic but the driver managed to pick up his passenger's address. When he emerged on the North side of the river imagine the driver's horror when he glanced over his shoulder and noticed that the pillion was empty! He turned round and drove back through the tunnel (there was only one in those days) but could find no trace of the hitch hiker. The next day the motor cyclist drove to the address he had been given and gave a description of the young man who had been his passenger. He was told the boy had been dead for some years!

72. Exit of pedestrian tunnel under the Thames on Isle of Dogs.

It was first enclosed in 1443 and many of the brick walls surrounding it date from the early 1600's. The park was best known in the last century however for its fair held at Easter and Whitsun. The fair attracted the common people who wanted to abandon themselves in drink and frolicking to escape—albeit for a short time—from their harsh lives. They would arrive down the river in steamers and along the roads in cabs, hackney-coaches, coal wagons, gigs and donkey chaises. It would be the equivalent of a South American Carnival and Dickens who went there analysed it as:

> "a periodical breaking out we suppose; a sort of rash; a three days fever which cools the blood for six months afterwards".

The fair attracted prostitutes, footpads and swindlers with all sorts of fancy costumes and sideshows. Rope dancing, fortune telling and balloons were among the more modern attractions and there were probably dog and cock fights taking place with much betting. One tradition of the Greenwich fair was for young men to walk their loved ones to the top of the hill and taking their hand pull them down as fast as they could go 'greatly to the derangement of their mobs and bonnet caps'.

73. Young men pulling their loved ones down Greenwich hill.

There was a great deal of feeling against the fair and many sought to have it surpressed, this finally being achieved in 1857.

74. Anne Boleyn: Executed for alleged incest.

Nearly every school pupil, at least of my generation, has heard of Sir Walter Raleigh laying down his cloak over a muddy puddle so that Queen Elizabeth I would not dirty her feet. Raleigh was later to lay down his head as we shall see. How many people know that this noble deed was carried out at Greenwich, near the river? It was at about this time that Sir Francis Drake docked just down the river at Deptford after the first circumnavigation of the world. Greenwich played an important role in the life of the Tudors. Henry VIII, Queen Mary and Queen Elizabeth were all born here at Placentia the Pleasant Palace, a Palace which was the former home of Henry VI, though it no longer stands today. It was in Greenwich that Henry VIII trumped up charges against his second wife Anne Boleyn. He was seeking ways and reasons to be rid of her and whilst at Greenwich she was seen to drop her handkerchief, this supposedly being a sign to her lover. She was beheaded for alleged adultery with several men, one of whom was her own brother. Her body was not to rest however and her troubled figure has been seen many times since she was executed in 1536 on Tower Green. This might in some ways be explained by the fact that a coffin was not provided and she had to be buried in an old arrow chest. Anne asked to die by the sword rather than the axe so a French executioner was hired for the event. He was dressed entirely in black with a mask, contrasting with the red robe worn by the ex-queen.

75. Sir Walter Raleigh.

64

Anne Boleyn's ghost has most often been sighted near the Tower and just over one hundred years ago the Captain of the guard saw a light from inside the White Tower and climbed a ladder to witness the following spectacle taken from 'Ghostly Visitors' by 'Spectre Stricken', London 1882.

"Slowly down the aisle moved a stately procession of knights and ladies, attired in ancient costumes; and in front walked an elegant female whose face was averted from him, but whose figure greatly resembled the one he had seen in reported portraits of Anne Boleyn. After having repeatedly paced the chapel, the entire procession, together with the light, disappeared."

A guard at the Tower in 1864 challenged a white shape that appeared in the mist; when it did not heed his warning he fixed his bayonet but the ghost passed right through. The man's story was believed and corroborated by two other guards who witnessed the proceedings, all believing this was the ghost of Anne Boleyn. Anne made her final journey down river to be executed and her barge has been witnessed on the Thames on several occasions.

Greenwich is not short of a ghost or two of its own and one of the most spectacular sightings has been that of Lord George Angerstein who haunts Trafalgar Road in Greenwich. He is collected from the Ship and Billet Inn and transported to his old home by a coach drawn by four headless horses. Perhaps the most famous ghost is that of Admiral Byng, executed for treason in 1757 and still protesting his innocence. He was shot on board the Monarque after being confined in a small top-floor room in the South East Pavilion of the Royal Naval College. He had much time to reflect on his actions and many people today consider him to have been unjustly sentenced. It seems he is still around to help convince any doubters. The ghost manifests itself in many ways; a filmy figure, and a sinister shrouded presence which disappears when addressed and mysterious footsteps have been heard.

76. Apparition—A Victorian Fake.

One of the most amazing photographs of a ghost ever taken was shot in the Queen's House, Greenwich. The Kodachrome transparency of a shrouded figure on the stairs was taken by a Canadian clergyman and is certainly the most convincing photograph I have ever seen.

There seems to be one or maybe two figures climbing the stairway, the picture being taken from a low position.

Besides its ghosts Greenwich has a great deal to offer. You can visit the Gypsy Moth IV in which Sir Francis Chichester sailed single-handedly around the world. He was once asked if he had witnessed anything of the supernatural on his travels he replied that he had had a most terrifying experience but would not enlarge upon the details. He probably took the secret to his grave. The clothes Nelson wore at the Battle of Trafalgar are in the Museum and you can also visit the Observatory where Halley (of the Comet fame) worked for many years.

Other famous figures spending time in the area include Bob Hope, Edgar Wallace, Geoffrey Chaucer, General Wolfe and General Gordon.

77. Admiral Byng executed by firing squad, 1757.

GREENWICH LIFE IN 1884

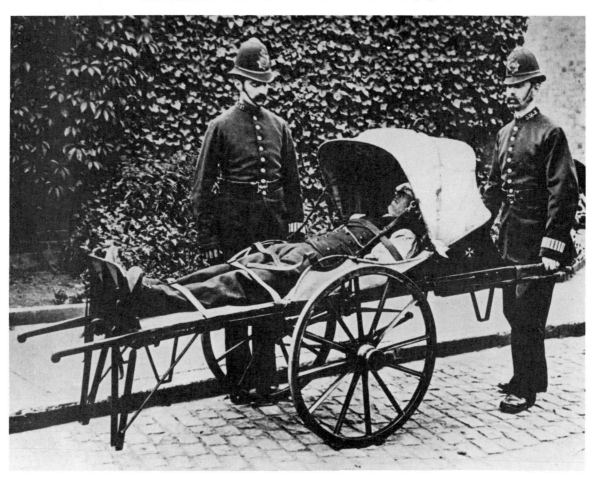

SCENES OF GREENWICH 1884-5

1. The Police in 1885 were also trained in First-Aid.

2. Hokey-Pokey. The ice-cream of 1884 was turned out in the foulest conditions and responsible for more epidemics than anything else except milk and water.

3. The Muffin Man. The bell and cry were welcome sounds in working class homes just before dusk.

4. The Match Makers trade was a killer, the yellow phosphorus giving rise to the disease "Phossy Jaw" and premature baldness.

5. SW-EE-EE-P! By 1884 the act of sending young boys up chimneys had been abolished.

6. Sherbet and Shrimps were a popular treat for the youngsters of the day. Note the boys lack of shoes and womens arthritic fingers.

THE CUTTY SARK

The first sight of Greenwich for many of its two million visitors a year is the spectacular view of one of the most graceful ships ever to sail the seven seas: The Cutty Sark, a famous Clipper now restored to her former glory and in dry dock on the banks of the Thames.

Built in Scotland in 1869 she was to become one of the fastest Clippers ever to be built, making frequent runs to India, Australia and later, America. Her achievements have been noted in many articles. There are however one or two stories handed down by the crew over the years showing that life aboard was not without incident, some of it unexplained.

There were frequent reports of sailors on the Cutty Sark seeing phantom ships and the more superstitious would run towards the ship's figurehead for protection (incidently the hull is now full of figureheads). One of the sailors on his first voyage on the ship made a model of her in a bottle.

After its completion the ship hit exceptionally high seas and bad weather and during the storm twenty sailors saw an enormous five-masted sailing ship bearing down on them at an incredible speed. The sailor threw the model over the side at the same time a gigantic wave engulfed the ship. Emerging, to everyones astonishment and relief, the five-masted sailing ship had vanished without trace.

The ship has also been the scene of at least one murder. In 1890, carrying a load of coal to the Far East, the mate after losing his temper, killed one of the seaman. He somehow managed to escape aboard an American ship. The captain of the ship was so unsettled by these events that one night he just slipped quietly over the side and was never heard of again.

A new captain was appointed but he eventually turned to drinking and giving fire-and-brimstone services to his crew.

After a spell with the Portuguese Navy and as a training ship for boys she finally settled in her permanent home, the dry dock at Greenwich.

PRISON HULKS/DEPORTATION

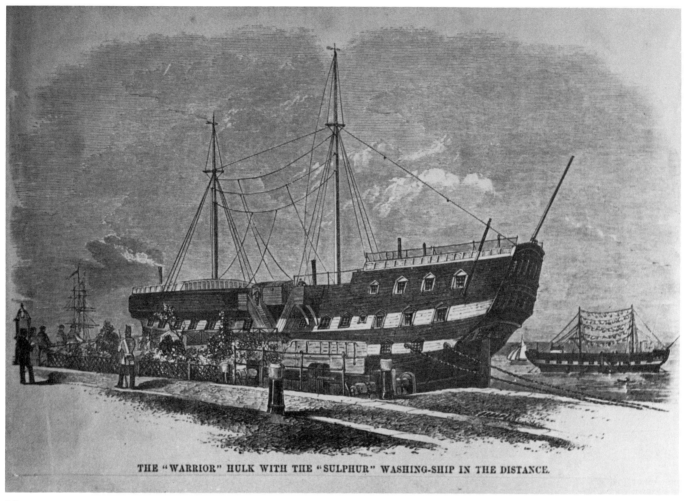

THE "WARRIOR" HULK WITH THE "SULPHUR" WASHING-SHIP IN THE DISTANCE.

85.

One day as we were a-walking
A gentleman passed us by;
I could see she was bent on some mischief
By the rolling of her dark blue eye.
Gold watch she picked from his pocket
And slyly placed into my hand;
I was taken in charge by a copper,
Bad luck to that black velvet band.

Before the Lord Mayor I was taken,
'Your case, sir, I plainly can see,
And, if I'm not greatly mistaken
You're bound far over the sea'.
It's over the dark and blue ocean,
Far away to Van Diemen's Land,
Way from my friends and relations
And the girl with the black velvet band.

Two verses from the nineteenth century ballad 'The Girl with the Black Velvet Band.'

As long ago as the Elizabethan age there were discussions as to what to do with the surplus population of the capital, the beggars, drunkards and petty criminals. It was proposed that they be sent to the new world which was in need of manpower. It was not until 150 years later that the policy was put into practice and even death sentences were waived in favour of transportation for life. During the American War of Independence hundreds of prisoners were kept waiting on board ships until the British victory. As we all now know, they were to have a long wait.

These prison ships (old boats no longer seaworthy) were moored off Woolwich and Deptford and became known as the hulks.

The conditions on board were so bad that they became major tourist attractions with boat owners going down the Thames taking visitors as close as they dare go, it needing an Act of Parliament to deter this. The convicts on arrival were placed on the lower decks where the air was most foul and damp and over the years gradually worked their way to the top. Prisoners slept in hammocks in terrible conditions of overcrowding with an area 6 ft. by 18 ins. to call their home. Indeed when prisoners died the others threw his body to the ground and fought over his hammock, searching for any goods or money he had secreted. No convict was allowed to be without an iron on one or both legs. The linen or blankets were very rarely changed and there were no towels or combs on board.

John Wade wrote about the conditions from the inside.

'On arriving on board we were all immediately stripped and washed in large tubs of water. After putting on each a suit of slop clothing we were ironed and sent below. I soon met many of my old Botany Bay acquaintances who were eager to offer me their friendship and services—that is with a view to rob me of what little I had . . . . here a man will rob his best benefactor of an article worth one halfpenny'.

The prisoners were taken ashore to work carrying coal, breaking stones, cleaning drains and sewers and removing earth. It is no surprise that disease was rife; Venereal disease, the itch, scurvy, typhus, dysentry and cholera. During cholera outbreaks prisoners were not buried until there were at least six dead, the dead bodies being left on board and eventually interred in their chains, the handlers being afraid to touch them. Some bodies were given over to medical research and dissected, with the remains left lying about for days in pails. Those that were buried were often dug up by body snatchers and sold, being referred to as "things for the surgeon". One ship, a captured Spanish boat, The Retribution, caused the authorities many problems. The guards carried clubs, and violence, sodomy and severe punishment were part of everyday life. Insane prisoners were kept on board as it was considered they would receive worse treatment in the lunatic asylum. Sometimes convicts rose to positions of power on boats and terrorised other inmates. Many boats were completely corrupt with counterfeiting and gambling commonplace.

In the earlier days smoking was approved of as it helped to fumigate the boat. The prisoners also received an allowance of two pints of beer daily (it cost 5 pence per gallon).

It must say something for the general poverty of the time that many local workers were envious of the conditions enjoyed by the prisoners on the hulks. In 1841 there were 3,625 prisoners in floating prisons on the Thames. By 1857 there were none, the last hulk being burned at Woolwich and the prisoners transferred or transported, this time to Australia.

86. Religious service on board one of the prison ships.

87. Top deck of the "Unité" hospital ship, attached to the hulks at Woolwich.

Deportation to America — 'Might they not have hanged at home?'.

Deportation had long been discussed as a means of removing London's undesirables and it was first put into practice in 1655 with eleven convicted prisoners preferring deportation to 'the new world' rather than permanent departure from the old and by the 1760's 1,000 a year were making the journey across the Atlantic, many for minor offences, as you could be deported for stealing a bag of carrots.

In all, between thirty and fifty thousand went to the colonies—mainly Virginia, Maryland and the Carolinas—before the War of Independence. They were referred to as white or christian servants to distinguish them from the black slaves and sold from advertisements in Virginia newspapers.

> 'A choice parcel of ten servants and one woman to be sold on the ship, Lovely now lying at the wharf of the Widow Allen. Also very good Gloucester cheese at eight pence a pound'.

The English were treated as little more than slaves, as is shown in a letter written home by a girl transported to Maryland.

> 'What we unfortunate English people suffer here is beyond the probability of you in England to conceive. Let it suffice that I am toiling almost every day and night and then tied up and whipp'd to that degree that you'd not serve an animal. Scarce anything but Indian corn and salt to eat and that even begrudged . . . . almost naked, no shoes nor stockings to wear and slaving during the master's pleasure'.

The Americans were none too keen on the idea of deportation either, even though they needed the manpower and some even suggested that rattlesnakes should be transported back to England in return for the prisoners on the same principle—in exile they might lose their venomous nature.

Benjamin Franklin was very much opposed to these new 'immigrants' and said of them:

> 'The instances of transported thieves advancing their fortunes is extremely rare, but of their being advanced to the gallows, the instances are plenty. Might they not well have been hanged at home?'.

EXECUTIONS

"Bacon's not the only thing cured by hanging from a tree"

The IDLE 'PRENTICE Executed at Tyburn.

88. An Execution Day was a national holiday.

For hundreds of years there was no bigger attraction in the capital than the public execution. A kind of carnival atmosphere greeted the unfortunate victims, many spectators having stayed up drinking all night to be sure of a good view. All echelons of London life attended the executions with the gentry hiring rooms in houses overlooking the site of the execution or else taking their place in specially erected stands. Indeed as recently as 1846, the houses opposite Newgate prison were rented out for the day, at prices varying between twenty and fifty guineas. This was to witness the mass hanging of seven pirates who mounted the scaffold, as white as the caps placed over their faces so the crowd could not see their convulsions. The pirates ankles were strapped together before they were simultaneously despatched to the hereafter for the entertainment of over two thousand spectators; mostly women and apprentices given the day off work to witness executions.

In early days the convicted prisoner had to mount a ladder with a rope tied around his neck and was ordered to jump, this system later being replaced by a horse and cart which were whisked away leaving the prisoner suspended in mid-air. The crowd would surge forward to pull the legs of the prisoner to ensure a speedier death. Many women dashed forward to place the dead man's hand on their cheeks or breasts as the dead were thought to have mystical gifts and be able to cure warts, pimples and other blemishes. After executions the rope would be sold at 6d a yard in a Fleet Street pub.

89. Women used to think that the touch of a dead man's hand would cure warts and other blemishes.

There are several interesting stories of people who managed to survive the drop. John Smith hanged for between five and fifteen minutes (the estimates vary) when a reprieve for his burglary came. He was immediately cut down and later recovered saying that the most painful part of the ordeal was the blood returning to his veins. At least two men survived in the same century (18th), one waking up on the surgeon's table, the other forcing open the lid of his coffin. A surgeon in Gough Square near Fleet Street purchased for the purpose of disection the body of a man hanged at Tyburn. A curious servant girl in his employment could not resist the temptation to have a peek at the body. Imagine her horror on entering the room to find the 'corpse' sitting upright. She fled downstairs in great haste to tell her master who, taking pity on the man, concealed him in the house until he could have him sent to America. A story stranger than fiction is concluded by the man making a fortune in the 'New World' and upon his death leaving it all to the doctor. On one occasion five men were reprieved at the last possible moment but had to walk home naked as the executioner had claimed their clothes.

It was not unknown for hanged men still found breathing on the anatomists table to be banged on the head by the surgeon so he would not be deprived of the body for dissection. One man who found more kindly surgeons was a 16 year old rapist and murderer, William Duell. Despite having shown no signs of life on the way to the surgery, Duell was found to be breathing on the surgeons table after being hanged earlier in the day. As an experiment the surgeons tried to revive him and in a short time he was sitting up drinking warm wine. He was returned to Newgate prison where he stated that hanging had not been painful, bringing only peace and unconsciousness in the midst of a beautiful dream. He was later transported to Dixie-land.

Next, a description of the execution of Charles White at Newgate, 1827. Camden Pelham, Chronicles of Crime, 1887.

The accustomed signal having been given, the drop sank; but the wretched man, instead of falling with it, suddenly jumped upon the platform, and seizing the cord around his throat with his hands, which he had sufficiently loosened by the violence of his struggles, he made an effort to prolong that life to which he seemed so strongly attached. At this moment the spectacle was horrible in the extreme. The convict was partly supended and partly resting on the platform. During his exertions his tongue had been forced from his mouth and the convulsions of his body and the contortions of his face were truly appalling. The cries from the crowd were of a frightful description, and they continued until the executioner had forced the wretched man's hand from the cord and having removed his feet from the platform had suffered his whole weight to be sustained by the rope. The distortions of his countenance could even now be seen by the crowd, and as he remained suspended with his face uncovered, the spectacle was terrific. The hangman at length terminated his sufferings by hanging to his legs, and the unhappy wretch was seen to struggle no more.

There were many valiant attempts to resuscitate the prisoners who had hanged the statutory half an hour. The associates of a certain Dr. Dodds used a double bellows to try and bring him around. Air and alkali were mixed and pumped into the lungs with spirits of hartsorn held over the bellows air inlet and the spine and oesophagus were pressed and massaged. Blankets were held near the body but were not allowed to touch it whilst steam of hot basalm circulated and was forced up his anus. Peppermint water, horseradish juice and turpentine water were applied though all in vain, the doctor not recovering consciousness.

Suspected prisoners sometimes refused to plead because if they were found guilty their property and possessions were handed over to the state. To combat this one of the most cruel punishments was devised to help extract a plea—'peine forte et dure'.

Judges would pass orders for the prisoner *'to be taken back to the prison from whence he came and laid in some low, dark house, where he shall lie naked upon the earth without any litter, rushes or other clothing, and without any raiment upon him save barely sufficient for decency; and he shall lie upon his back with his head covered and one arm shall be drawn to one quarter of the house with a cord, and the other arm to another quarter, and in the same manner let it be done to with the legs; and let there be laid upon his body iron and stone as much as he can bear and more; and the next day following he shall have three morsels of barley bread without drink, and the second day he shall have drink three times, as much as each time as he can drink of the water in the prison. And this shall be his diet until he die'.*

Sometimes the prisoners' relations were allowed to place a sharp stone under his body so death came more quickly. Pressing was abolished in 1772.

90. One of the many mass hangings.

91. *The New Gallows in the Old Bailey.*

92. *Satire on public executions.*

THE EXECUTION AND CONFESSION OF
FRANZ MULLER,
For the Murder of Mr. BRIGGS, November 14th, 1864.

At two o'clock on Saturday afternoon Sir George Grey returned an answer to the memorial presented to him, praying for a respite of the convict Muller, by the German Legal Protection Society. Previous to the delivery of his decision he had a long conversation with the Lord Chief Baron Pollock and Mr. Baron Martin, which terminated in his arriving at the conclusion that the memorial did not warrant his interfering with the verdict of the jury.

Immediately upon the receipt of the letter, Mr. Beard, with Alderman Wilson, proceeded to communicate to Muller the result of the efforts that had been made on his behalf. They were received by Mr. Jonas, the governor of Newgate, who conducted them to the condemned cell. They found the prisoner engaged in writing. He immediately rose, and extended his hand to Mr. Beard, who asked him how he was. The convict said, "I am very well." Mr. Jonas then informed the prisoner of the efforts that had been made to save his life, and that Mr. Beard had just received a reply from the Secretary of State, which he read to him. At the conclusion the convict said, in a low voice, "I did not expect anything else." Mr. Beard then said to the prisoner, "Did you know that any efforts had been made on your behalf?" The prisoner replied, "Yes, I did think so." Mr. Beard then said, "Have you any statement that you wish to make?" The prisoner, "No, nothing." "Because," continued Mr. Beard, "now that all has been done that can be done for you, and there is no hope in this world, if you have anything to acknowledge, you had better do so." In reply to this Muller said, "I should be a very bad fellow if I had done it. I have no other statement to make than that which I have already made." Mr. Beard then asked him if he had made his peace with God. The prisoner said, "Yes;" and in every respect appeared resigned to his fate. Mr. Beard then shook hands with him, and said, "Good-bye Muller; God bless you;" The prisoner returned the pressure of his hand, and was left to himself.

The prisoner on Sunday attended Divine service in the chapel, both in the morning and the afternoon, and listened apparently with deep attention to the discourse delivered by the Rev. Mr. Davis, the Ordinary. He was visited in the evening by Dr. Walbaum and Dr. Cappell.

PREPARATIONS FOR THE EXECUTION.

Up to Sunday night Muller preserved the same quiet, firm demeanour, and although he occupied some of his time in writing, he did not lie down till considerably after his usual time, and slept but little. He rose at five o'clock on Monday in good spirits, and was soon afterwards joined by the Rev. Mr. Davis, the chaplain of the gaol, and the Rev. Mr. Walbaum. He in every respect appeared calm and resigned to meet his fate. He joined devoutly in prayer with the rev. gentleman, and otherwise conducted himself in a manner becoming his awful position. A little before seven o'clock he was visited by Mr. Jonas, the governor of the gaol, to whom he extended his hand, and feelingly thanked him for the kind attention he had received since his incarceration. Calcraft arrived at six, but was not recognised by the mob, and thus escaped the usual hooting.

Although the fixing of the scaffold was completed by four o'clock, still the clang of hammers in putting up barriers continued till day had dawned.

At five o'clock a heavy drenching rain set in, which had the effect of driving the majority of those who during the night had taken up positions, from their strongholds, and to hastily beat a retreat to the now open public-houses and coffee-shops, as well as to other places offering anything like shelter. At this time there could not have been more than five hundred people actually upon the scene. But at six o'clock the rain abated, and from this time the crowd was recruited by an increasing flow of new comers.

At six o'clock the main body of police, under Mr. Inspector Duddy, was stationed at the approaches to, and in the Old Bailey, and preserved throughout the morning in the strictest order.

Soon after seven o'clock, Mr. Alderman and Sheriff Besley, Mr. Alderman and Sheriff Dakin, and the Under Sheriffs, Messrs. Davidson and De Jersey, arrived at the Sessions House, where they remained until summoned to the prison by the governor. About twenty minutes to eight they were informed that the condemned man would soon leave his cell. Upon receiving this intimation these officials left the Sessions House. A few minutes after this, the procession reached the door which opens into the chapel-yard. Here they awaited the arrival of the culprit.

THE EXECUTION.

While the officials were on their way from the Sessions House to this spot, Mr. Jonas had gone to the cell of the prisoner, and informed him that it was time for him to leave. The prisoner, who was deadly pale, trembled with emotion, but sought to bear the awful announcement with all the fortitude possible. He rose up, shook hands with the gaolers who had been principally with him since his incarceration, and with a firm and rather quick step left his cell, accompanied by Mr. Jonas, followed by two or three other officials. As soon as they left the cell the shouts and cries of "They are coming," "They are coming," "Hats off." At this moment the most intense excitement and confusion prevailed, in the midst of which terrible din reverberated the echoes of the solemn knell, which, from its increased rapid tolling, indicated that the mournful procession had gained the steps of the hideous, cloth-draped gibbet. A moment afterwards Calcraft, the hangman, made his appearance on the scaffold, and then withdrew to see that all was right. He had no sooner disappeared than Muller, accompanied by the Rev. J. Davis, chaplain, and Dr. Cappell, followed by other officials, made his appearance. This was a signal for the renewed excitement and clamour of the swerving multitude, who had largely, and as it were imperceptibly increased, and whose up-turned anxious faces met the gaze at all points.

The culprit ascended the scaffold with a firm step, and placed himself under the drop. He cast his eyes once up towards the beam, and his lips quivered with emotion, but this he evidently sought to check. After the cap had been drawn over his head and the rope put round his neck, Dr. Cappell took hold of his hand and again prayed with him. This he did for some minutes, and concluded by addressing the following words to the now fast dying man:—"In a few moments you will be before your God. I ask you, for the last time, are you innocent or guilty?"

Muller: I am innocent.

Dr. Cappell: You are innocent?

Muller: God Almighty knows what I have done.

Dr. Cappell: Does God know that you have done this deed?

Muller was silent.

Dr. Cappell: I ask you now, solemnly, and for the last time, have you committed this crime?

Muller: YES, I HAVE DONE IT.

Almost at the same instant, and while the words were upon the lips of the wretched man, the drop fell, and Muller died without a struggle.

Dr. Cappell nearly fainted.

Immediately after the execution the sheriffs despatched a communication to Sir George Grey, informing him that the culprit had confessed. A similar communication was made to Sir R. Mayne, at Scotland-yard.

The following despatch was immediately after the execution forwarded to the Home Secretary:—

"Gaol of Newgate, 14th day of November, 1864.

"To the Right Hon. Sir George Grey, Bart.

"Sir,—By direction of the sheriffs I have the honour to acquaint you that the prisoner Muller has at the last moment, just before the drop fell, confessed to the German minister of religion attending him that he was guilty of the deed for which he suffered.

"I have the honour, &c.,

"SEPTIMUS DAVIDSON, one of the under-sheriffs."

London : Printed for the Vendors.

93. Confessions were sold on sheets like this after an execution.

94. *Jack Shepherd.*

An even more famous burglar turned highwayman was Jack Shepherd whose notoriety has been spread over the centuries as a dashing fearless rogue who led the authorities a merry dance. Even a hundred years after his death his exploits were well-known and admired by thousands of London's street children, even though they could not read or write. He was above all famous for his daring escapes. A small wry man with a head for heights he specialised in lock picking. He was manacled and chained to the floor at Newgate prison but managed to slip out of the handcuffs and with a crooked nail opened the padlock that fastened the chains. He then set out on an incredible escape journey opening lock after lock, many of which had been rusty for years.

There is a fine line between fearlessness and stupidity and a few days after his escape Jack was to be seen strutting about Drury Lane, a short distance from the prison. He cerainly did not try to keep a low profile, wearing a black suit, wig and a ruffled shirt, diamond ring on every finger and a gold watch in his waistcoat pocket. He was eventually recaptured blind drunk.

The public heard of his escape and daring and he became something of a cult figure, being visited in prison by hordes of admiring women and even some prominent politicians.

Jack was not going to meet his maker without a struggle and he secreted a penknife about his person, hoping to cut the rope on the way to the gallows; the knife however was discovered. The cart he rode in was showered with flowers from an admiring public. Even as the noose was tightened around his neck Jack had not played his last card. His friends were waiting to pull him down and revive him. It was thought they were going to run forward as he dangled to pull at his legs but in reality, they intended to support him. Because of the mass of people this plan did not work. There was a surgeon in attendance and when Jack was finally cut down his friends tried unsuccessfully to resuscitate him with hot blankets and bleeding. Jack Shepherd was twenty-three.

At executions the prisoners were brought from prison, usually Newgate, in a cart, the front seat being occupied by the hangman 'Jack Ketch'. There may have been other passengers in the cart but if the prisoner had been convicted of treason he would be forced to ride backwards. Many of the women would be dressed all in white and would scatter oranges and flowers to the crowd from the cart en route to execution. It was one of the perks of the executioner to be allowed to keep the clothes of the victims. At one hanging there was uproar when Hannah Dagoe brawled with the executioner who tried to stop her stripping off and throwing her clothes to the crowd. She was an immensely strong Irish woman who threw her gloves, bonnet and cardinal to a friend. She cursed the hangman daring him to hang her and one of her blows was so strong she nearly knocked him out of the cart. She was eventually to depart the world exactly as she arrived.

The crowds were not always hostile to the prisoners and there was a great deal of sympathy for highwaymen, especially if young and attractive. One of the knights of the road much admired by the ladies was Jack Rann who once appeared in court, his irons decorated with blue ribbons, sporting a bunch of flowers in his coat. He received the name of sixteen string Jack after wearing eight different coloured "strings" on each leg of his knee-breeches. The prospect of death didn't seem to frighten Jack a great deal as on the eve of his execution he entertained a number of his admirers to dinner at Newgate. He went out in style too, wearing a pea-green suit and a huge nosegay on his button-hole.

95. *Catherine Hayes burnt for the murder of her husband (from the annals of Newgate).*

96. The bodies of those executed were anatomised over a period of three days.

Highwaymen were an exception to the rule and most people on their way to the gallows experienced the wrath of the crowds. They were verbally abused and often pelted with bricks and dead cats. One of the most hated men ever to go to the gallows—and one instrumental in the conviction of Jack Shepherd was a certain Jonathan Wild. He was both a receiver and informer and allegedly responsible for the conviction and eventual execution of over seventy malefactors. He used to ride in front of the convicted prisoners announcing that his children were coming. He was hated by the London mob and when he was finally convicted, took laudanam and went to the gallows in a semi-comatose state. He was pelted with anything the crowd could get hold of and they demanded a very quick death. It is reported that Jonathan Wild picked the pocket of the priest on the scaffold and held the watch up to the crowd. Two days after burial his body was dug up and sold to the Royal College of Surgeons and the skeleton, with excellent teeth but trepanned skull, can still be seen today.

More than the hanging itself, prisoners would worry what would happen to their bodies afterwards, fearing they would be anatomised. After execution many of the bodies would be brought to the surgeons hall and dissected in front of the fee-paying spectators. These dissections would last three days, and at the end of which a banquet would be held and what was left of the bodies hung in an alcove.

Hanging was not the only form of capital punishment and poisoners were boiled alive, while witches were burned and strangled simultaneously. Many of the more famous

98. Pirates were hanged at Wapping.

historical figures were beheaded near The Tower and the most guilty and worthy of death were hanged, drawn and quartered. Tyburn was closed as a place of execution in 1783 because of the ever increasing problem of riots associated with the hangings.

The King's ships captured me as I sailed, as I sailed,
The King's ships captured me, as I sailed,
The King's ships captured me, no more of piracy,
And no more to own the sea, as I sailed, as I sailed.

Now to Execution Dock I must go, I must go,
To Execution Dock I must go,
To the Execution Dock, put my head upon the block,
And no more God's laws I'll mock, as I fall, as I fall.

Take warning now by me, I must die, I must die,
Take warning now by me, I must die.
Take warning now by me, and shun all bad company,
Lest you go to hell with me as I die, as I die.

These three verses are from the broadside published on the occasion of the execution of Captain William Kidd for murder and piracy in 1701.

97. Religious Martyrs were often burned.

THE HANGMEN OF LONDON

99. *The identity of the executioner of Charles I is still unknown to this day.*

'Prithee let me feel the axe. I fear it is not sharp enough'

Despite being possibly the most hated position in England, the post of public hangman was much sought after, the incumbent being paid a piece rate. In times of turmoil he was rarely without work and during the ten year reign of James I, 1,472 people were put to death in London and Middlesex. The hangman was also responsible for floggings, beheadings and burning at the stake. In extreme cases of treason he was also charged with hanging, drawing and quartering the traitors. In this last form of death, a fire was lit as the man was hanging and—still barely alive, he was cut down, his head severed with a cleaver and disembowelled, the heart and entrails being cast into the fire. Sometimes as many as nine people were executed at the same time so we can see it was not a job for the faint-hearted.

All hangmen since 1686 have been known as Jack Ketch after the executioner of that name who had occupied the post for twenty-three years. He had a record of incompetence and savagery and one of his executions was described by a witness at the time:—

'The hangman gave him three blows, besides sawing with ye axe, before he cut his head off'.

A further example of Ketch's bungling concerns the execution of the Duke of Monmouth, still a very popular figure after his unsuccessful rising. The scaffold of Tower Hill was draped with black cloth and rather than kneeling the low block was used, the victim having to lay full length. The Duke was very composed and his final words were a request to the incompetent Ketch:

'Prithee let me feel the axe. I fear it is not sharp enough'. Ketch brought the axe down too lightly inflicting only a wound. Monmouth raised his head and turned to look him in the face before resuming his position. Ketch struck a second and third blow, both being ineffective before throwing down the axe crying;

'God damn me, I can do no more! My heart fails me'.

He was made to continue and after two more blows he still had to sever the head with his knife. The crowd was incensed, many crying. The bungling Ketch was removed from his office soon after in 1686. Ketch was not the only executioner to bungle his job. One hangman's name, Derrick, has passed into the English language, meaning 'a hoisting apparatus employing a tackle rigged at the end of a beam'. Derrick was attacked by the London mob after he had taken three blows to remove the head of the Earl of Essex. He had been particularly insensitive as, after the Earl, dressed all in black save a red waistcoat, had laid down and fitted his neck into the block, he had ordered him to stand up again lest his doublet might obstruct the axe.

Not a great deal is known about the executioners before this time and even the identity of the axeman charged with cutting off the King's head in 1649 is in dispute. The hangman at the time of Charles's execution was named Brandon and he said publicly that he would not carry out the execution. There were unsuccessful attempts at bribery and a troop with horses sent to collect him in order to perform the execution. The two executioners on the scaffold were both masked and it is not known who actually wielded the axe though Brandon died some five months later. His body was buried in Whitechapel and written on the gravestone were the words:—

'21st Rich Brandon, a man out of Rosemary Lane'.

Added later in a different hand were the words:

'This R. Brandon is supposed to have cut off the head of Charles I'.

100. *The execution of Charles I 1649.*

Executions were never so popular as when Jack Ketch himself was to undergo the treatment he had meted out to so many poor wretches. Many of the executioners were drunkards or in debt or involved in petty crime and John Price, the Jack Ketch of 1715, was convicted of murder. He was taken to the scene of his crime in Upper Moorfields through a vast crowd of jubilant women cheering with delight. Dressed in a white shirt and holding a nosegay he protested his innocence, but on the scaffold finally admitted to the crime of murdering an old stall keeper in a drunken stupor.

His body was later hanged in chains upon a gibbet as a warning to others. The character and modus operandi of the various state executioners varied greatly. Some used the long drop, often breaking the victims neck; others used just one or two feet of rope, the death through strangulation taking considerably longer. The crowd in general did not like to see the convicted prisoner suffer and the Jack Ketch's were booed and threatened if they did not do a clean job. Different executioners had different personalities. There was a smiling Jack Ketch in the first half of the nineteenth century who tried to put the victim's mind at ease and others who displayed no sympathy whatsoever for their victims.

John Thrift, the Jack Ketch in 1750 was taunted by a mob outside his house shouting out 'Jack Ketch, Jack Ketch'. He ran out into the street, cutlass drawn, and murdered one of his tormentors. He was sentenced to transportation, but he never left the shores and was pardoned and eventually returned to his old job.

At least two hangmen were haunted by the ghosts of their victims. The assassin of Spencer Percival, the only British Prime Minister to have been murdered in office, was John Bellingham who was executed six days after his crime. Even though the hangman had been doing his job for twenty-six years and must have killed and flogged hundreds of men and women he seems to have become unhinged after hanging Bellingham, the victim coming back to haunt him in his dreams.

The executioner in 1923 was named Ellis who had taken the lives of over two hundred prisoners. He, along with everyone else present at the execution of twenty-eight year old Mrs. Thompson was to be affected for the rest of his life by the memory of that day. Mrs. Thompson was convicted of murdering her husband and on the way to the gallows Ellis said he 'saw her disintegrate as a human being'. He later attempted suicide and kept seeing the poor woman's ghost. Every official present resigned; the chaplain fell seriously ill and the wardress mentally unhinged.

101. *Bodies were exhibited in gibbets as a deterrent (from the London Dungeon).*

102. *Execution of Lady Jane Grey at the Tower of London.*

There are stories of the sons of executioners taking their father's place after serving their apprenticeships on dogs and cats and also a case where a man named Derrick was sentenced to death for rape in Calais and pardoned by a nobleman whose head he later cut off after taking up the appointment of chief executioner.

The hangmen were universally detested by the lower orders and took their lives in their hands every time they performed their duties. Indeed, one executioner, Marvell, was pounced on by the crowd on the way to Tyburn and kidnapped. A substitute hangman had to be found, but when one of the crowd volunteered, he was pounced upon by the rest of the mob and nearly beaten to death. Needless to say no one else volunteered, despite the promise of a large reward. The three convicted prisoners were taken back to the condemned cell and their sentences later commuted to penal servitude. It is thought they may have been transported to the Carolinas but one at least came back and was later hanged for another crime. Marvell had been instrumental in one of the most spectacular beheadings which attracted a large crowd. The victims were Lord Derwenter and Lord Kenmere, both young and attractive men convicted of being traitors. Derwenter gave Marvell a gift of several guineas so he would perform a clean job and showing no signs of fear knelt down to see if the block would fit his neck. He said his prayers and gave the signal to chop by saying the words 'sweet Jesus' three times. His neck was severed by one terrific blow. Two blows were needed for the second victim, Lord Kenmere, who had given Marvell a present of eight guineas. Marvell the executioner was dismissed and fell into a life of poverty and petty crime.

FAMOUS LAST WORDS

We have witnessed the calmness with which Monmouth and Raleigh went to their execution by their demeanour and their last words. Although there is no connection with London, the last words of those to be executed (most of them in the U.S.A.) are of a certain bizarre human interest.

'I'll guess the Big Bad Wolf is going to get me'.
    William Dene in Pennsylvania.

'I'll see you all in hell some day. Let 'er go!'.
    Jesse Thomas.

'The soup I had for supper tonight was too hot'.
    Charles Fithian.

'Tell them in the kitchen to fry Glenn's eggs on both sides, he likes them that way'.
        Irene Schroeder alias Iron Irene or Tiger Girl.

'Well folks you'll soon see a baked Appel'.
    George Appel in the Electric Chair.

'I'm Jack the ......'.
        Neill Cream, a man suspected of being Jack the Ripper. The trap door opened before he could complete his sentence.

THE TOWER OF LONDON

"I am not here to preach to you but to die"—Anne Boleyn

The Tower has been one of the most versatile of buildings since it was originally built by the Normans to awe the local population into submission after the Battle of Hastings. It has been used as a Palace, prison, place of execution and has housed the royal armouries, the mint, the royal observatory, the public records and today, still guards the Crown Jewels.

The Tower was probably London's first Zoo and in its time has held Elephants, Leopards, Lions and Bears. A Polar bear was kept on a long chain so that it could feed itself by fishing in the Thames. James I delighted in the combats of wild beasts, mostly lions and bears being baited by dogs. There was a most barbaric competition in which a bear was sentenced to death after killing a small child. Lions were put in the same pen to carry out the sentence but were too afraid to approach the grizzly. It was eventually baited to death by dogs.

Keeping in the same theme of animals, there is a strange exhibit in the Tiger Tavern which is connected by an underground tunnel to the Tower itself. If you can go to the upper bar you will find the mummified remains of a cat which is supposed to have been stroked by the young Queen Elizabeth whilst still a prisoner in the Tower. Every ten years, the Lord Mayor of London comes to the pub to test the beer. Some beer is poured onto a stool and the beer-tester invited to sit; if his trousers stick to the seat all is well and a laurel leaf is hung outside the door and a garland round the neck of the landlord.

103. The Tower today.

Elizabeth is just one of the many famous prisoners held in this top class penitentiary. Prisoners were held here as recently as World War II with the imprisoning of Germanys number two, Rudolf Hess after his still unexplained parachute jump into Britain during the last War. Sir Walter Raleigh spent many years of his life imprisoned here on three different occasions. He was first interred for eight weeks for 'winning the heart' of one of Elizabeth's maids of honour. He was later imprisoned and sentenced to death for plotting to place Arabella Stuart on the throne. He was reprieved the day before his execution was due and spent the next years in comparative luxury with his wife and son in the Bloody Tower. Here he wrote his famous 'History of the World' and devoted himself to his chemistry. He was released some fourteen years later to lead an expedition to America but this was not successful and he was re-arrested and later executed. He showed no fear of death whatsoever and on the way to his execution gave a richly embroidered hat to an elderly balding man saying:

> 'Take this, good friend, to remember me, for you have more need of it than I'.

He added just before his execution:

> 'I have a long journey before me . . . .'

And touching the axe he commented;

> 'This is a sharp medicine but it will cure all diseases'.

Raleighs last words to the hesitant executioner were;

> 'What dost thou fear? strike man!'

Raleigh's ghost is still to be seen haunting an area now known as Raleigh's walk.

104. Richard III: Did he order the murder of the princes?

To list all the prisoners held in the Tower would be like compiling a historical 'who's who' but one of the most famous murders of British history was carried out here and the identity of the perpetrator of this horrendous crime has never been conclusively proved; The murder of the Princes in the Tower will continue to give rise to controversy among historians for many years to come. In 1483, one month after the coronation of Richard III, two young Princes, Edward V (12) and the Duke of York (9) were killed in the Garden Tower which was henceforth known as the Bloody Tower. Very little is known about the actual details but it is thought they were murdered by two men named Green and Forest who were acting on the Kings orders. There is, however, a Society for the defence of Richard III still active today, who say he had no hand in the plot. Exhumation in 1933 of two bodies buried in Westminster Abbey suggest they were the two young Princes whose bodies had originally been found in Charles II's reign under a staircase.

Despite holding some of the most famous characters in history, a stay in the Tower was relished by few. There were some luxurious cells but also those which could feature in any horror film shown today. If you feel your hotel room is a little on the cramped side why not try 'Little Ease', one of the rooms at the Tower. This was a hole under the White Tower behind a small door with an iron grating at the top. It was just eighteen inches wide, four feet high and two feet deep. Prisoners would have their heads forced down on their chests and be unable to sit or lean in this private hell. After a spell here you might be forced to sit on a heated stone until you confessed, or put into a cell which was later flooded and infested by famished rats. When the tide rose, the cell filled with stinking water and hordes of hungry savage rats. These had to be fought off in the dark and after a period of time the prisoner became weary and fell prey to the sharp teeth of the rodents.

The Tower is locked and bolted every night at 22.00 hours with the ceremony of the Keys and no stranger is allowed in after this time. It will come as no surprise to the reader that probably more ghosts have been seen here than anywhere else in the world.

Spies and traitors faced the firing squad here in the Second World War and in recent times a Yeoman Warder has noticed a strange figure dressed in 1940's Utility suit appear near the firing range. The figure disappeared as the Warder tried to get a better view, and in 1954 another Warder saw a puff of white smoke coming from one of the ancient cannons. This smoke drifted towards the Warden, changing shape as it did so, the story being confirmed by a second guard.

Ghosts are by no means twentieth century phenomena and one of the Tower's oldest is that of Sir Thomas Becket. A room has been dedicated to him at the Tower after he was seen in 1240 and in this room the doors open and close without reason and ghostly footsteps have been heard. The figure of a Monk in a brown robe has also been spotted.

The sinister shadow of an axe passing over Tower Green and finally settling on the White Tower, where it becomes clearly defined, is reputed to be connecterd with one of the most savage executions ever to take place here, that of the Countess of Salisbury, who was over seventy but still had a very strong will to live. She was sentenced to death on religious grounds by Henry VIII but she refused to put her head on the block and was pursued screaming around the scaffold after escaping her guards. She was pursued by the executioner who caught her and threw the lady to her knees. He missed his target three times and gashed the defiant lady's neck before finally severing her head.

The Tower is still not a safe place today, in the Martin Tower in the last few years visitors have felt unseen hands trying to push them down the steep stone staircase. It is thought that the culprit might be the man who caused the guards to work in pairs, a certain Thomas Percy who was imprisoned here for his part in the abortive gunpowder plot.

Probably the Towers most famous resident is Anne Boleyn and the story of her appearances is told under the section on Greenwich, but her brother is also in residence here after being hanged, drawn and quartered. He may be found at the North Eastern quarter of the Inner defence works, the Martin Tower.

The Tower today is one of London's major tourist attractions and certainly worth a day of anybodys stay even if they hold only a mild interest in history—beware on the stairs!

105. One of the many forms of torture used over the centuries at The Tower (from the London Dungeon).